STARTUPS MADE SIMPLE

How to Start, Grow and Systemize Your Dream Business

BY MATT KNEE

Copyright © 2019 by ROCKNEE LLC

All Rights Reserved.

No part of this book may be reproduced in any form or by any electronic or mechanical means, including information storage and retrieval systems, without written permission from the author, except for the use of brief quotations in a book review.

This book is provided with the understanding that neither the publisher nor the author are engaged in rendering legal, tax, financial or other services nor are they engaged in rendering professional advice to the individual reader. Neither the author nor the publisher shall be liable or responsible for any loss or damage allegedly arising from any information or suggestion in this book.

All product and company names are trademarks ™ or registered ® trademarks of their respective holders. Use of them does not imply any affiliation with or endorsement by them.

First Edition: January 2019

ISBN
Paperback: 978-0-578-44598-4

TABLE OF CONTENTS

Acknowledgements iv
Introduction 1

PART ONE: The Founder Superpowers

1. Energy 14
2. Vision 24
3. Execution 30
4. Leadership 61

PART TWO: The 6-Step System

5. Step One: Imagine It 92
6. Step Two: Plan It 112
7: Step Three: Start It 129
8. Step Four: Grow It 155
9. Step Five: Manage It 171
10. Step Six: Systemize It 222

PART THREE: The Scorecards

The Founder Superpowers Scorecard 238
The 6-Step Scorecard 239

Conclusion 243
About the Author 244
Appendix 245

ACKNOWLEDGEMENTS

I would love to say that I personally invented, conceived of, or developed every strategy, tactic, habit and system in this book. The truth is that there's very little new information or secrets in how businesses are started, grown, or managed and I'm ruthless and shameless about implementing anything that works, regardless of the source. I've even joked that this book is a "well-organized theft of ideas." Many of these are other people's ideas that I've distilled, simplified, and repurposed to serve the startup entrepreneur. If I have any skill whatsoever, it's condensing and organizing complex information, then making it simple for others to understand and implement.

Because many of these ideas originated with other people, I've listed them in the Appendix and within the book itself. I'm a voracious consumer of information, so my fear is that I've integrated these concepts, books, and ideas into my life and business so much over the past 17 years (in an enormous digital library of quotes, documents, clippings, etc.) that it's hard to tell which ideas are mine or from where they originated. If I may have left someone out as a source, I apologize in advance and will happily update this book with any clarifications or sources.

My next fear is that I'm going to forget someone in the upcoming list. These are the individuals I've known—or followed their work so closely over the years it *feels* like I know them—that have taught, mentored, coached, worked with, or otherwise helped or inspired me:

STARTUPS MADE SIMPLE

- Allan Dib*
- Bart Patterson
- Bill Theisinger
- Chris Mershon
- Dalton Hooks
- Dan Glavin
- Dan Kennedy*
- Danila Shabalin
- David Allen*
- David Chavez
- Eric Ries
- George Garcia
- Gino Wickman*
- Jay Abraham*
- Jeffrey Decker
- Jeremy Curran
- Jim Collins*
- Michael Gerber*
- Michael Kwan
- Naval Ravikant*
- Paul Graham*
- Peter Drucker*
- Ricki Reynolds
- Rob Atlas
- Robbin Turner
- Sam Carpenter*
- Steve Blank*
- Verne Harnish*

*These people have books or writing I highly recommend and list in the Appendix.

Finally, I'm eternally grateful to my customers and employees over the years, business organizations I've belonged to (YEC, Vistage, Velocity Circles), my family (especially my mom who was employee #1 at my first company), and my wife, who continues to be my most trusted advisor (and editor).

Startups Made Simple is not about the hottest new management theory; it's about imagining your dream business and making that a reality with step-by-step implementation and skills that have been proven to work time and time again. I hope you enjoy it, and most importantly, actually implement these ideas so you can enjoy the wealth and freedom that having a great business allows.

INTRODUCTION

What Is the Purpose of this Book?

Imagine the perfect business for you. Imagine that you could take that vision and systematically, in clear simple steps, make it a reality while saving time and avoiding the mistakes that destroy most startups.

Creating a business is the greatest source of personal freedom, wealth and progress in the world. Nearly three-quarters of the Forbes 500 Richest People are on that list because they own a stake in one or more businesses. And the majority of those people are "first generation" — they didn't inherit the wealth, they created it.

I believe the future of humanity's progress will be led by entrepreneurs. Think of all the entrepreneurs working on everything from space exploration, renewable energy, easier ways to get a cab, or even a better or faster meal. These people are making the world a better place through their business. This is the power of entrepreneurship: You can create fantastic wealth while helping people and even help solve the world's problems.

This book is a guide to take the entrepreneur from an idea to a real, profitable and systemized company (one that allows you to take a real vacation) as fast and easy as humanly possible. My intention is to make this book the best and most concise guide for entrepreneurs starting a business in the real world; especially for those without a lot of resources and connections.

This book deals very little with pitching investors, going to conferences, or other things that are popular with "wantrapreneurs" who seem to do everything but actually build a business. My focus is on the bootstrap entrepreneurs that start real businesses every day. In reality, less than 1% of startups get venture capital funding.

Silicon Valley types like to disparage these small businesses as a "lifestyle business" with "only" $1 million dollars per year in revenue or less. It's amazing; they'll congratulate you for *raising* $1 million in funding but not actually *making* $1 million in revenue. However, most of these small business owners work damn hard and deserve the freedom that a well-run business can provide.

Silicon Valley also seems to be obsessed with writing books, articles, and more about best practices that only seem to apply in hyper-competitive, well-funded businesses that basically have a monopoly (Google, Microsoft, Facebook, etc.). Many of these companies are nothing like 99.9% of businesses in the real world. For example, most small business owners just need good, reliable employees that show up on time. These small businesses cannot afford stock options, catered lunches, free daycare, massages, personal development training and the many other things required to compete in the ultra-competitive job market of Silicon Valley and other tech hotspots.

There are also literally thousands of small business books available on Amazon and other places, but what I've found is that the vast majority of them 1) over-complicate things, usually so they can sell you their consulting or other services, and 2) should not be books at all. They should be articles because the concept is simple and the author has padded the information with endless stories and examples to make it book length.

These are huge pet peeves of mine, so I hope to avoid both issues in this book by presenting the information clearly, minimizing fluff and filler, and providing clear and simple action steps and checklists every step of the way because I assume you're as busy as any CEO. Minimizing wasted time and unnecessary risks for a startup is the entire point of this book. This is the book I would give my friends and family to most ensure their success.

Why Listen to Me?

I founded MyCompanyWorks, Inc., from my apartment with less than $1,000 in 2001. This was in the middle of the "dot com crash" and one month after 9/11, so the economy wasn't exactly what I would call optimal. Since then, we've helped over 50,000 entrepreneurs start their business. In that time, we've never taken a loan or venture capital, never had an unprofitable year, and have been honored to make the Inc Magazine INC5000 fastest growing companies in America list.

More importantly, I've made almost every mistake in the book (and continue to make mistakes!). There's nothing special about me except perhaps my intolerance and embarrassment over screwing up so much. I've left millions of dollars on the floor and have damaged relationships and my health because of the many poor decisions I have made through the various phases of my company. I don't want you to make the same mistakes.

I also personally know many successful entrepreneurs and have spoken to thousands of them as our clients about their successes and failures. I consider this topic to be my wheelhouse and constantly devour any information I can find on startups and small business management.

Let Me Be Your Guide

This book contains the distilled wisdom from my experience and that of many others. More importantly, I'm obsessed with what makes a startup succeed and how to simplify this into a system that can be replicated.

There are many companies that are much larger, make more money, and have a greater impact on the planet than mine. But, one of the things I emphasize in this book is that you want to start the perfect company for *you*, not what others expect or want. It's silly to want anything else.

I'm perfectly happy with my business the way it is and would hate anything much more complex or "corporate." I don't like constant meetings, complex business models, or a difficult-to-manage business. But that's just me.

Today, my business is systemized, requires little supervision, and grows consistently. I choose when to work or go on a vacation when I want, and I'm in the best shape of my life.

The business continues to generate income and wealth while I am free to work on the big-picture projects or not work at all, depending on my mood. In my opinion, wealth, freedom, and making an impact or helping other people via your business is a peak life experience, an experience I'd like to help others attain.

Why Businesses Fail

Unfortunately, the statistics for new business startups are pretty grim. Depending on the source of data, you can expect at least a 50% failure rate within a few years (these statistics are more or less the same worldwide). Some sources place that number as high as 90% after 10 years. In addition, 96% of businesses never break $1 million per year in revenue. These startups never get past a few employees because the entrepreneur is in their own way and doesn't plan, communicate, or systemize.

One thing I've noticed is that there are many ways to succeed in business. You can succeed via a good plan, lots of funding, a great idea or product, luck, good timing, good economy, connections, or many other things (usually combinations of those things). However, it seems that one big key to success is simply not making the big mistakes that seem to be common among startups.

So, instead of focusing so much on what you need to do to succeed in your startup, we're starting to find out that a lot of doing well in business (and life in general) is simply avoiding the bad habits, decisions and situations that have continually proven to lead to bad results. Basically, it's easier to learn from the mistakes of others than it is to make all those same mistakes yourself. This concept is called *via negativa* (popularized by the book *Antifragile* by Nassim Taleb) and I use it frequently throughout this book to make you aware of the well-known startup and small business management mistakes.

Personally, I've made a number of huge mistakes that have wasted a lot of time, energy, and money, literally millions of dollars as I've mentioned. Sure, I've learned from them and they were valuable lessons but some were easily avoidable with even a basic amount of planning and preparation.

If you're going to start a business, you might as well do some quick planning now to save you hundreds of hours of heartache down the road. Don't over-plan, but don't go into the process blind. The great thing about business is you can attempt as many times as you want, but you only have to succeed once to be set for life.

Don't Believe the Hype

There are a lot of misconceptions about startups these days. For example, did you know that the average age of a successful startup founder is 45? From all the hype you see in media, you would assume all the successful founders are barely out of high school or in their 20s. As I'll show you in Part One of this book, there are founder skills that are critical to success and older people tend to have acquired more of these skills over time.

Or did you know that of those 90% of businesses that failed, up to one-third of those businesses were actually profitable? Yes, just like anything else, a founder can become tired of their business and might have simply closed it, sold it, or moved on. This dramatically changes our perception of the 90% failure rate mentioned above. The reality now seems to indicate a real failure rate of a bit higher than 50%, and I'll take a 50/50 shot every time.

Armed with those facts, a startup doesn't look so daunting now, does it? What I want to do is add valuable planning, skills, and habits to the equation, and I believe this will dramatically improve your chances for success. Merely being aware of some of the landmines and best practices for startups should be incredibly helpful.

Why Planning is Important

Here's the nightmare scenario: You've started your company, it's making money, you're working hard, and decide you really need a vacation. The problem is that the company is entirely dependent on you; you couldn't take a vacation or even a sick day if you wanted.

Suddenly, you realize that you haven't created a company, you've only created another job for yourself—with no paid time off! Even worse, you are 100% responsible for everything and your customers are now your boss. You now have more pressure and stress then you did when you worked for someone else and are probably wondering what the point was. Trust me, I spent years like this.

This is not an uncommon scenario. The vast majority of entrepreneurs are stuck in their business working on the day-to-day, and they work, on average, well over 50 hours per week. They don't realize that they're actually the bottleneck in the growth and systemization of their company. Whether you're just planning or have already started your business, I will show you a clear way out of this trap.

Many books like the *E-Myth* and others have covered this topic, but the basic truth is that most people know a skill or craft but don't know how to build or manage a proper business with systems. Franchises like McDonalds and 7-Eleven almost always succeed because they have a system and an operations manual for each new franchisee/owner to follow step-by-step and has been proven to work.

Systems = Freedom

System is the key word here. Systems are the key to your freedom and will multiply the value of your company because it will not be completely dependent on you. I not only show you how to do basic planning from the very beginning, but how to lay down a framework for you to eventually replace yourself as your business grows—not to mention that systemizing a business is an incredibly valuable skill to learn and apply elsewhere.

A business that does not have systems is in a difficult place.

This "owner dependent" type of business usually hits crisis when the founder gets sick or needs to retire or sell the business. So, even if you don't intend to be more than a one-person company or don't intend to sell your company, I make the argument that you should at least have basic systems in place, if only for your own sanity. At the bare minimum, keep everything in the same place and some basic instructions for loved ones if there is some kind of emergency.

Worst case scenarios aside, one thing I want to emphasize is that by "planning," I don't mean a 50-page business plan and a 200-page operations manual. Modern business planning focuses on speed, simplicity, and testing your idea before you do an enormous amount of planning — the plan I give you fits on one page.

In the real world, most companies are started with more of a shotgun approach to validate the idea and get moving. Someone starts a website, a person starts charging for their shirts or consulting, etc. This has largely replaced complex business plans because the focus is on getting quick market validation so you can correct course quickly and not spend months and lots of money on a bad idea.

Also, we won't be building out a huge operations manual but will instead simply start documenting things in one document and let you organize things organically and systematically from the start. If you already have a business, then we'll show you how to begin organizing things as well.

Using this system, you should be able to grow your business to $1 million in revenue and potentially a lot more depending on the complexity of your business. Every business is different. We keep the system simple for people at that level and below. Once you exceed several million dollars in sales, then the complexity of your company will grow and may require additional systems, but I want to emphasize again that, while you should plan, there is no need to overplan and over-optimize things until you get to that level.

Overview and How to Use This Book

This book has three parts. **Part One** covers what I've found to be the skills and habits of great founders that I call The Founder Superpowers.

In **Part Two**, we dive in to the system, which has six steps:

1. **Imagine it**. Whether you have a business idea in mind or not, this section will help you brainstorm and clarify your idea. We also work on a vision for the perfect business for you. Having a clear vision of what you want is the first step to making it real.

2. **Plan it**. Using a simple one-page plan, we begin laying out what you need to test this business idea and then get it off the ground as quick as possible.

3. **Start it**. An overview and simple checklist of things to do to get your business registered and legal. We also cover picking the business name, entity, taxes, and more.

4. **Grow it**. Using another simple plan, we lay out the steps to help you identify your ideal customer to build your "sales machine" and grow your business.

5. **Manage it.** We cover the five things you need to master to have a well-run business: the plan, process, people, tools, and routines.

6. **Systemize it.** We put it all together and systemize your business into one simple system and continue simplifying and improving your business until it is essentially self-running.

Part Three contains two scorecards to assess your skills as a founder and assess your company as a whole. I recommend you complete them after reading the book to get a baseline score. Everything in the first two parts should help you dramatically improve in these areas.

Feel free to skip around if you are in a hurry or already have a business and need specific help in any area. Otherwise, I believe the book is brief enough to go from beginning to end, skimming what you already know. I use bullet points and checklists extensively and each section or chapter has resources for implementation.

Now that you know what to expect, let's dive in and keep the following tips in mind:

- Take the time to go through the book and do the action steps. These things done properly should save you many hours of painful "make up work" later. It's amazing, but most people will put more planning into their wedding than their life or business! Do a few hours of planning to massively clarify your thinking and build a business right, a few hours to save hundreds later. Thinking through important things for a few hours will put you ahead of 99% of the population on earth.

- My writing style is very direct and informal and can sometimes come across as "tough love" or even a bit harsh despite my best intentions. This is because I'd rather give you the real truth about business instead of some motivational nonsense that should be on a business poster (which is what I see a lot of in business books these days).

- Note that the **Imagine it** step can be applied to a new business or to reimagine your existing business (I've done this a few times, and we're on our third company name!), to brainstorm a new product or just solve some problems you have at your company or in life.

- We'll start with one document I call the Startups Made Simple Planner. We'll work with this planner from idea all the way to systemization. This document will be a godsend later in business, trust me. Download a free Startups Made Simple Planner at www.StartupsMadeSimple.com and make sure to keep all of your company startup and planning documents, plans, and notes together in one folder (either a real folder/binder or on your computer).

Feedback and Resources:

Website: www.StartupsMadeSimple.com
Email: info@startupsmadesimple.com
Twitter: https://twitter.com/mattknee

Onward!

PART ONE

The Founder Superpowers

"I see entrepreneurial efforts often fail but good entrepreneurs don't fail."
— Naval Ravikant, founder of AngelList

Why do we start with the founder habits, skills, and traits that I call the Founder Superpowers? Because these have proven to be the most obvious determining factors of success in starting a business. Highly effective founders can make even mediocre ideas work and bad teams more effective. It's why venture capitalists and others keep shoving piles of cash at the same people over and over: These people have a set of skills that continually deliver results.

Habits and skills, however, can be learned, and through my research over the years, there is a core set of skills that will definitely improve your odds for success. Don't worry if you don't have all of these right now (and I would never insinuate I have all of these). People succeed all the time without some or even most of these skills. However, they are usually *very good* at one or more of these and have a cofounder, team, or at least an assistant that compensates for a lack of any of these skills. (Or they simply learn them on the fly like most of us.) Think of all of these as a "talent stack" as *Dilbert*'s Scott Adams likes to say; the better you get at each one adds value because they all work together.

The Superpowers

I group these superpowers in four broad categories:

Energy:

- Superpower #1: Health
- Superpower #2: Perseverance
- Superpower #3: Optimism
- Superpower #4: Momentum

Vision:

- Superpower #5: Clear Vision
- Superpower #6: Clear Goals
- Superpower #7: Product Obsession

Execution:

- Superpower #8: Agency Mindset
- Superpower #9: Resourcefulness
- Superpower #10: Personal Productivity
- Superpower #11: Good Decisions
- Superpower #12: Problem Solving

Leadership:

- Superpower #13: Good Communication Skills
- Superpower #14: Accountability Mindset
- Superpower #15: Team Development and Motivation
- Superpower #16: Courage to be Disliked

These categories might sound like an oversimplification, but think about it—if you have enough **Energy**, you can work very hard on whatever you put your mind to for as long as necessary and persist through tough times. If you have a clear **Vision**, then you can imagine a clear future and something great that people will want. If you are great at **Execution**, then you can get things done, including implementing your Vision. Now combine all this with **Leadership** and the ability to get a team to go along and get things done, then you're basically unstoppable in life (not just business).

Note that these could also easily be called the Employee Superpowers in many regards, so developing these skills in your team is a great way to build a great company. You can make a team of highly competent, entrepreneurial, mini-CEOs.

In Part Three, I provide a checklist for you to rate yourself (and your co-founders or team might consider doing this) on these Superpowers, which should help you not only improve in areas where you are weak but focus on areas where you are strong.

1
ENERGY

When I talk about Energy as it relates to startups, I'm giving it a broad definition to include not only your physical health but also your mental health and things like perseverance, the mental toughness required to get you through the rough spots of being an entrepreneur.

Superpower #1: Health

"The first wealth is health." —Ralph Waldo Emerson

Say there are two founders that have the exact same set of skills and knowledge but one is healthier than the other. Nine times out of ten, the healthier founder will outperform the other. Healthy founders simply have more mental and physical energy to bring to bear on the various issues that a startup encounters, not to mention they will be sick less and able to bounce back faster from setbacks. You want to prioritize your health and energy first, which will allow you to be more effective in almost every aspect of your life.

It's critical that the founder not make the mistake of overworking and ignoring their physical health. Trust me on this. It's almost a badge of honor how much founders work, but I'm of the belief that founder who works 40 hours a week but is well-rested, "clocks out" at night, takes proper vacations (even if just a 3-day "staycation" around the house), eats healthy, and most importantly, sleeps well, will easily outperform a neurotic founder who works 60 hours a week but doesn't do these things. There's much more on this in later chapters.

Remember: It's not selfish to focus on your health. It's actually moral and responsible for you to make sure you're healthy enough to make sure your company survives and thrives, especially when others are counting on you.

Mental Health

Taking care of your mental health is as critical as your physical health (perhaps more). One thing I've noticed is how many of the "rock star" entrepreneurs and successful people I admire have worked on their mental game as much as their physical game.

In the book *Tribe of Mentors* by Tim Ferriss, nearly 80% of the successful people he interviewed have some form of meditation or relaxation practice. Arnold Schwarzenegger and billionaire hedge fund manager Ray Dalio have credited mindfulness meditation for much of their success. Being able to calm your mind is an incredibly valuable skill and has been a game changer for me personally. I list resources on this in the Chapter Resources.

Another aspect of mental health that affects a lot of founders is "imposter syndrome." Imposter syndrome is very common among many high-performing people, and is where you feel like a fraud, feel that you don't know what you're doing, and fear that you'll be exposed as a fake.

Trust me, this is very common and comes from the fact that you're usually pushing yourself to learn new things as you grow your skills. Life and business never provides 100% certainty. When I learned that many world-changing geniuses and entrepreneurs also felt like this, it was an enormous relief.

One interesting thing is that pretty much nobody fully knows what they're doing, and while that might be terrifying (my first thought: what about pilots!), it's actually pretty relieving. By the way, pilots have lots of training and sophisticated help via a backup pilot, air traffic controllers, weather, and flight software, so as we discuss later, having systems and a team you trust will help in your startup journey.

A lot has also been written recently about loneliness and depression among founders. I'd be lying if I said that these things have never affected me or founders I know. If you're a founder, you're probably going to encounter times where you feel absolutely alone and nobody else really understands or cares, even your best friends and family. It's not that they don't want to help; it's that they likely can't possibly understand your specific situation at this time, and that's totally normal.

Connecting with other founders locally and online is a great way to overcome loneliness. There are now so many communities, organizations, Facebook groups, Twitter personalities, and more that the "startup ecosystem" is now very big and supportive. In the resources section of this chapter, I list some great resources for connecting with fellow founders that can make this journey easier. Actually, one of the reasons I've structured this book in such a systematic manner is to overcome a major reason for depression: being overwhelmed and not knowing what to do next.

Hopefully, by breaking down this process into bite-size chunks, we can take some of the overwhelm out of the process. Taking care of your physical health is a big part of fighting depression. Finally, never be ashamed to admit you're depressed to your doctor, friends and family, and get the help you need.

Superpower #2: Perseverance

> *"I'm convinced that about half of what separates the successful entrepreneurs from the non-successful ones is pure perseverance."* —Steve Jobs

> *"Nothing in the world can take the place of Persistence. Talent will not; nothing is more common than unsuccessful men with talent. Genius will not; unrewarded genius is almost a proverb. Education will not; the world is full*

of educated derelicts. Persistence and determination alone are omnipotent. The slogan 'Press On' has solved and always will solve the problems of the human race."
—*Calvin Coolidge*

I've noticed the best entrepreneurs are known for their perseverance; they can be trusted to get through the rough stuff. So many of the great tales in business and in life are about the person who simply did not give up, even after many obstacles and setbacks. Resilience, persistence, grit, tenacity, confidence, and relentlessness are related traits, and in general, overcoming fear is a big part of perseverance.

In my opinion, people have been taught to quit way too quickly. Scammy marketing and advertising has conditioned many of us to expect fast or even instant results. The truth is that many skills take years to develop. Some things as simple as a handstand can take many months of daily practice to master, yet the majority of people give up in a few weeks or if they can't find a program called "Mastering Handstands in Only One Week!"

This doesn't mean it will take years to learn how to get your company going; it only means that you shouldn't immediately give up if you're not performing like Elon Musk in the first year of your startup. Some startups, the smart ones anyway, may take a year or two to work on their idea, test things in the marketplace, quickly pivot to another product or service, and continue learning from their customers. There will be much more on this in Part Two of this book, and there is such a thing as going on too long. Mostly, the problem lies with giving up too early.

For now, just know that your first instinct, especially when things get tough, may be to quit. Quitting sounds so comfortable (for lack of a better word) when things are bad. I wanted to quit several times in the first couple of years for, in retrospect, completely ridiculous reasons.

Make sure that if you're thinking about quitting that you're not closer to victory than you think you are. A lot of entrepreneurs quit on the ten-yard line right before they are about to succeed. This is so common that it's almost legend now. I'm asking you to carefully consider when you feel like giving up. I've learned that some days are just going to be a "shit sandwich," and you have to take a bite. You will have bad days or maybe even bad weeks, and a perseverance mindset will help you greatly.

Also, business is not nearly as hard as some stories out there about people sleeping in their cars or having nervous breakdowns. In fact, I think a lot of successful entrepreneurs like to embellish their startup stories to motivate their teams and create a hero's journey for the startup. (I'm certainly guilty of that myself on some occasions.)

However, the business world can be competitive and you can be pushed around if you're too sensitive or thin-skinned. You want to develop a thick skin and also hire other people who have thick skins. In my opinion, overly sensitive people are typically not fit to be in a startup environment. A lot of business is about not being intimidated by partners, employees, customers, or vendors.

I've found a stoic outlook can be best for getting through the rough patches. Winston Churchill once said, "If you're going through hell, keep going." I've also learned that in business "they can't eat you" (customers, vendors, competitors, employees, etc.), so some days you have to just smile at the absurdity of worrying about things as if they're life or death and try to have a good time with it all.

Finally, there is such a thing as having too much perseverance; a good entrepreneur knows when it's time to quit. This may not always be obvious to us, but a very good indicator is when the product or service is not getting any traction despite your best efforts.

In these cases, you don't have to admit defeat; only acknowledge that you don't like working for free and the market is firing you—for now. In Step 1 of this book, you'll see how this has happened sometimes dozens of times to great founders and is not something that should discourage you.

Remember it's all a Game

> *"One of the symptoms of approaching nervous breakdown is the belief that one's work is terribly important."*
> —Bertrand Russell

In reality, it's all a big game, and you can't take any of it with you in the end (regardless of your religious beliefs), so really take some time to consider that you don't need to take any of this stuff too seriously. If you can take care of your physical and mental health while persevering through it all, you'll do great.

The universe is inconceivably large, billions of years old, and you're a tiny organism on a spinning rock orbiting a random star in one of billions of galaxies. Even if your work was actually world-changing and important, the universe would barely notice. Genghis Khan or Caesar were little more than a infinitesimal blip in the universe, and taking yourself too seriously is a great way to be miserable. This is not meant to depress you or to say your work doesn't have meaning, but to provide perspective for you to remember that all you have is this life now, so do what you can to give it meaning for you and try to have a good time.

Superpower #3: Optimism

> *"Optimism is a force multiplier."* —Colin Powell

I'm sure there are successful founders who are not optimistic—I've just never met one. Seriously though, an optimistic mindset is a huge source of energy, and the good news is that optimism can be learned. (See the Chapter Resources for more information.) Pessimistic and negative people are usually not only low energy themselves, but they tend to drain the energy of everyone around them. Pessimism is the last thing a founder needs in the startup process.

Think about it, have you ever met a pessimistic "Debbie Downer" who was a successful businessperson—or successful anything? I cannot think of one example outside of perhaps a few "artist" types that used negativity in their artwork. Otherwise, every inspirational business book or biography inevitably has an incredibly optimistic person behind it, and I don't think that's a coincidence.

Note that I'm not advising you to not be realistic; you can be realistic *and* optimistic. I've joked that optimism is worth twenty extra IQ points because you don't immediately give up. When you have optimism, you give your brain permission to look at the bright side of things as they happen and see possibilities that a pessimist may have rejected or not even thought about.

That's exactly how an entrepreneur needs to deal with the inevitable curveballs that will be thrown at them. They need to realistically assess the situation and see if there are any solutions to mitigate the problem, change the situation to their advantage or, at the very least, learn a valuable lesson. An optimistic mindset and many of the other superpowers in this part of the book will help you move away from pessimism and toward solving problems, which is what great founders primarily do.

Superpower #4: Momentum

Hopefully you're starting to see how critical energy is, and how you can use it to your advantage. Anyone who has watched a sports event where a team comes back from behind and then dominates knows exactly what I mean by momentum; you can feel it in the air. It's one of the best sensations in business and life, and I highly recommend you use it to fuel your startup. Momentum supercharges energy.

So, how do we build momentum? As you are probably starting to realize, all these superpowers work together in many ways. As we'll see later, having a great Vision and learning to Execute will create momentum, which is infectious, your team will naturally be motivated by your momentum, just like the sports team example above.

The reason why I separated it out as a superpower is that I just want to make sure you recognize the power of momentum and use it to your advantage. You'll feel it typically as a gut feeling and possibly a rush of energy that may last hours or weeks. Use it! Sometimes, I'll only hit a good surge of momentum once a week or even once every few weeks, but one thing I never do is waste it. I know when I'm in the zone and use that momentum to get a massive amount of things done, push big projects forward, get things done around the house, or even knock off a bucket list item. (You can use momentum for fun!)

One final tip I have concerning momentum is to try to preserve a little so you can reignite it the next day. I'm somewhat infamous to those who know me for being able to work 18 hours in a row on a project or idea. While that allowed me to get great things done when I was younger, there was always an inevitable crash afterward. The older, wiser me knows that I should cut out after the momentum begins to fall off a bit and simply reignite it the next day, letting my brain work on it and continue being excited while I sleep.

Energy Best Practices

Having plenty of Energy is usually a matter of doing some very basic things but I realize a lot of this goes out the window while doing a startup. Here are some best practices:

- **Good sleep**. Prioritize sleep above all as your main source of energy and renewal. Sleep at least 7 hours (and more if necessary) and make sure you practice proper sleep hygiene (minimize blue light at night, cool room, no noises, etc.). There are many good sleep apps, trackers and even special beds and "light blockers" available to optimize sleep.

- **Clean diet**. Most startups are run on a consistent supply of donuts, pizza and other junk and while this is fine occasionally, you'll want to keep your diet as clean as possible to maintain an ideal weight and to provide plenty of energy. Consider intermittent fasting which is getting very popular among high-performing people as a source of energy and clarity.

- **Exercise**. We all know we should do it so make exercise a priority. Even jogging around the block or bodyweight exercises at the office are helpful and a big key is finding an exercise routine you *like* doing. Realize that exercising actually gives you *more* energy, improves sleep and optimizes mood.

- **Purge negative energy**. Negative people, thoughts (negative self-talk) and media should be removed from your life as much as possible. You want to remove anything that drains your energy including abusing alcohol or drugs.

- **Emotional self control**. Work on becoming thick-skinned and "highly undisturbable". I recommend a few books in the Chapter Resources.

- **Sunlight**. More data is coming in every day about how important sunlight and your vitamin D levels are for overall health and energy. Get plenty of sunlight, have your vitamin D levels checked regularly and supplement or use a light therapy device to resolve any issues.

- **Supplement**. Get a regular panel of blood work for the various markers of health and supplement accordingly. Apparently, vitamin D, magnesium, iodine, omega-3 and other nutrients are at historically low levels across the western population and can usually be resolved with simple supplementation. I list some tests in the Chapter Resources.

- **Meditation or relaxation.** As mentioned, a huge percentage of highly successful people have a regular meditation or relaxation routine. There are many books, apps and websites that make this ridiculously easy to learn and I list some in the Chapter Resources as well.

- **Sense of humor.** As discussed, it's all a game and you can't take any of it with you. Maintain a sense of humor, even in the face of bad situations and you'll tend to get through things just fine. Laughter is a powerful cure to many problems.

Chapter Resources for Chapter One:
http://www.startupsmadesimple.com

2
VISION

"Vision without action is a daydream. Action without vision is a nightmare."   —Japanese proverb

Vision includes not only the ability to see things clearly into the future, but also how you envision your company, including an obsession with building a great product. Those with great vision can often think ahead to where they want to be and reverse engineer the steps needed to realize their vision, starting with their next logical step.

Superpower #5: Clear Vision

Having a big or clear vision is almost synonymous with being an entrepreneur. Whether you think big with your ideas or not, you more than likely have a pretty clear vision of what you want. You want to develop this skill as much as possible by thinking in a very detailed way. Walt Disney didn't imagine your average county fair carnival when he imagined Disneyland; he dreamed up something magical.

Don't just think that you'll have a cool business in a few years; instead, write the very specific details of what it looks like, how many employees you have, what the offices are like, what you do all day, and how you feel. Get excited about this, and then make sure you clearly communicate this vision to your team. That's pretty much it for Vision. Think big, think clearly, and communicate this to everyone on your team. We'll go over this much more in Step 1: Imagine it.

The problem is that a lot of visionaries are procrastinators and are even worse if they think really big because they're paralyzed by the enormity of their vision. This is why you must focus on one idea and make it a reality via execution, which we discuss in the next chapter and why Part Two has six distinct steps to take you from idea to a fully systemized business.

Superpower #6: Clear Goals

Very closely related to Clear Vision is how you will reverse engineer your Vision into Clear Goals, concrete action steps that need to be taken to turn that Vision into reality. This is where most visionaries drop the ball and remain in the thinking part, not the doing part.

In a well-run company, not only is there usually one big, obvious goal (called a "Big Hairy Audacious Goal" or BHAG® made famous in the book *Good to Great* by Jim Collins), but you should have realistic (but aggressive) yearly and quarterly goals that you're looking to accomplish that moves your company forward to that big goal. Each employee should have an individual goal and that's usually (but not always) tied to the company goal.

For example, let's say my Vision was to build the next "LinkedIn for Businesses" platform and my BHAG was to have 1 million businesses on my platform by 2029. Here's how I might quickly brainstorm and reverse engineer the steps to make that goal. Note that these are just wild guesses and things will change each year or even quarter.

1. Write specifications for beta version of website

2. Design mockup and logo for website

3. Get a marketing list of 1,000 random small businesses of all types for testing

4. Build and test website

5. Invite marketing list for free beta signup and to provide feedback
6. Interview 10 users a week and build around their biggest feature requests
7. Launch "Invite my Address Book" functionality
8. Reach 10,000 signups
9. Launch targeted ads and newsletter functionality
10. Reach $10,000 in monthly revenue
11. Launch "Message my Business" functionality
12. Launch mobile app
13. Launch national digital advertising campaign
14. Reach 100,000 signups
15. Launch "Recommended Vendor" functionality
16. Reach $100,000 in monthly revenue
17. Reach 250,000 signups
18. Launch premium membership option
19. Launch national radio advertising campaign
20. Reach 500,000 signups
21. Launch national TV advertising campaign
22. Reach 1 million signups

Based on that very rough list of possible goals to get to our BHAG, you can close in on the likely goals you'll need for the next year or so and then further break down those goals by quarter. So you've taken a long term vision and now have a solid sense of what needs to get done in the next year. Now break down what needs to happen this year by quarters, make them measurable and assign them to a responsible person (likely yourself at first).

The important thing is to have the vision and general roadmap to getting there and adjust along the way. With this example, I know I need to get working on the specs and design for my website right away. Finally, assigning deadlines (even if those are guesses) to your goals is a very effective way to encourage their completion and add a sense of urgency to getting them done.

A frequent question I get is, "When am I supposed to find the time to work on goals while I'm busy working in my business?" The obvious answer is that building your business should already be based on clear goals, but if not, then you should make a roadmap like I've listed above. As I discuss in the section on the superpower of Productivity, there is Real Work and there is Process Work. Process Work is the stuff you do daily to provide your product or service. Real Work is working on Goals and things that move the company forward.

If your vision and BHAG are big, then realize you'll never get there doing the Process Work all day. I recommend you brainstorm goals yearly and assign goals each quarter to individuals and make sure they are measurable. We'll go into more specifics about creating a plan for your company in later chapters, especially Step 5.

Superpower #7: Product Obsession

Great founders typically have a very clear vision of how their business, product, or service should work, how their clients perceive and interact with their business, and include details on how the product looks and feels. Many founders work very hard on perfecting and even micromanaging the user experience from beginning to end and I believe this can pay huge dividends. You can truly tell when you're doing business that has a founder who cares about these things, usually from the moment you go into their business location or visit their website.

If there's a disconnect between a founder and the average employee, it's because many times an employee just doesn't "get it" in regards to creating a truly great client experience and having high standards (especially if the founder has not communicated the importance of that to the team). This is why I see a lot of people quit companies and start their own company; they have higher standards than their former boss or manager and believe they can definitely do it better.

The average employee may not understand that misspellings and bad spacing/formatting on website, emails, or marketing material are bad and reflect poorly on the business. Why broken signs, dirty bathrooms, and dirty counters look terrible and indicate sloppy management. Why the company name "DeBeers" is written properly and "Debeers" is not. Details matter.

Try to find any of the above-mentioned issues on anything that Apple does from their website to their retail stores to their emails; it simply doesn't happen, and that's because Steve Jobs made the user experience an obsession. If your employee doesn't understand why a misspelling or dirty counter is a huge deal, then that person needs proper training or needs to work somewhere else with lower standards. You usually know you have a superstar employee if they start noticing things that would drive you crazy and pointing them out, or better yet, fixing them.

If something in your business is allowed to go below your standards and is not fixed or noticed by anyone, then you actually have set a new standard whether you intended to or not. If employees *have* noticed it and have not done anything, then that's even worse, and you need to take action to make sure your standards are known and clear.

How to Build a Great Product or Service

1. **Focus on good design.** Whether you have good taste in design or need to hire a good designer for your product, focusing on good design is usually step one in building a great product. Note that designing a great process or service is design as well.

2. **Have written standards.** If how you expect things are not known, then how will your team know? Write these down

as policies, procedures, and even core value or mission statements. See Step 5 for more on this.

3. **Experience it yourself.** Actually use your own product or service like a client would (or have a friend or family member do this) and make sure you *want* to use your product (it's a big warning sign if you don't want to). Make this a regular habit and fix anything below your standards.

4. **Have a roadmap.** Write down exactly how your customer experiences your product, and examine the process from beginning to end for ways to simplify and improve the experience. Centralize and prioritize feature requests and improvements so you know where the product is going.

5. **Focus on the customer.** Be focused on the customer and what they want, not on what you want or what your competition is doing. Watch competitors, yes, but keep your focus on your customer and you can't lose if you listen to them and meet their needs. Keep a list of client feedback or complaints and fix the issues one by one.

6. **Provide superior service.** This is almost always the easiest differentiator when starting out, especially if your product or service is not up to your standards yet. You may not be able to offer a great product or low prices, but you can hustle on service. The advanced version of this is to build a product so great or intuitive that it doesn't require much service or that clients can self-service.

Chapter Resources for Chapter Two:
http://www.startupsmadesimple.com

3
EXECUTION

"You are what you do, not what you say you'll do."
—Carl Jung

The ability to Execute and get things done is probably one of the most valuable abilities a human can have. In business, it's absolutely essential, and if you can get things done, you will be handsomely rewarded, not only in business, but in life as well.

Hopefully you are starting to see how these superpowers work together. If you have a clear Vision and can Execute on that Vision, then you are an incredibly effective person. Add in Energy and Leadership (the next chapter) and the ability to get other people to execute, then you're basically unstoppable.

Superpower #8: Agency Mindset

"I shall either find a way or make one." —Hannibal

My favorite word for execution and the ability to get things done is Agency. Agency is a powerful word, but you've probably not heard it used in this manner. It's the skill that every venture capitalist is looking for and every employer as well. If you have Agency, then you can be trusted to get done almost anything that is capable of being done. Most important, Agency is taking 100% responsibility for your life and its outcomes.

If you have Agency, you can be given responsibility for something and the person who gave you that simply knows it will get done and done well. Pretty much all of the other execution habits are related to or tactics related to Agency. If you don't like fancy words like that, then a related concept is "Git'er done" made famous by comedian Larry the Cable Guy. It is the same concept: just get the job done.

Agency means I can ask someone to do something, and it will get done within reason. If somebody has Agency, you don't have to follow-up with them, you don't have to beg them for task or project updates (they'll proactively update you before you need it). Agency is taking ownership of the task and responsibility for getting it done right. Agency is doing even mundane tasks well.

Agency is what we want from presidents, generals, project managers, employees, assistants, partners, babysitters—almost anyone. If you want to get ahead in business, be respected by pretty much everyone, or improve your career, then become someone known for Agency. Finally, and perhaps most importantly, Agency means you take responsibility for your decisions and any consequences that result.

A big clarification: Agency does not mean hard work, and knowing the difference is critical. I always respect hard workers, but you have to know and reward the difference. My local landscaper works hard, the people at your local restaurant work hard, and people at your office may work hard. But an absolute critical distinction is that hard work, while admirable, is not necessarily getting the right things done that need to get done.

You can work insanely hard, but if you're not working on the right things, then hard work can actually be counterproductive. After you have hired and managed enough employees, you'll understand this critical difference. Some people can manage to be extremely busy all day yet accomplish half of what a person with Agency will accomplish in less time.

How to Build Agency

Here's the best part: Agency is a capability that can be called from within. I believe every person has Agency in them, they just need to light the fire.

Here's an example:

Imagine you are broke but you owe me $1,000. If I casually said I need that $1,000 in 6 hours, you'd probably dismiss this as not possible and tell me to pound sand or "I'll get it when I can."

However, if you are broke but need $1,000 in 6 hours for a life-saving medication for your loved one or they will die, it will get done.

It may require extraordinary energy, running all over town, calling, pawning, selling, begging, or even something illegal, but the point is that most people can call up the resources within to get this done. This is Agency, and if you place enough importance on a task, and as long as it's capable of being done, you'll get it done. Find it within yourself.

Another thing I've noticed with people that have Agency is that they have a very simple outlook on getting things done along the lines of Yoda's famous "do or do not, there is no try" statement. In many ways, it's almost a martial mindset; sometimes simple thinking is powerful thinking.

How do you lose weight? You eat less and exercise more. How do you get motivated? You wake up and start working on the most important task and motivation will come. How do you have that hard conversation? You pick up the phone and call the person or meet them.

There's something that needs to get done, and they do it. There's not a lot of over-complication or over-thinking in people with Agency, which is the curse of a lot of intelligent people and founders I've known.

Superpower #9: Resourcefulness

Next in line and closely related to Agency is Resourcefulness. As a founder of a startup with limited resources (and all but the most well-funded startups have limited resources), you need to learn a lot, stretch every dollar, do more with less, solve the big problems, land the big meetings or deals, and build the great product or service. Frugality is a related trait.

You will never have the resources to do everything you want, so you have to be Resourceful and figure out how to acquire the resources you need to succeed. Again, very similar to Agency but worth mentioning as all businesses are about prioritizing resources.

How to Build Resourcefulness

Admit to yourself that you will never have enough resources to do everything you want and that you must prioritize, make trade-offs, and use your existing resources as much as possible. Learn to make do with what you have at this time, and strategize to get what you need to take you to the next step in your plan.

Resourceful people look for answers and solutions themselves and don't need their hand held. For example, later I recommend you choose and use a digital calendar and task manager. Now, I could provide all kinds of recommendations, instructions, steps, and even step-by-step screenshots of how to set them up and use them. However, I promised not to waste your time and I'm going to trust that you're Resourceful enough to click "Help" on the website or app and read the most up-to-date information in learning these tools. When you have employees, you want them to be Resourceful too and not need constant hand-holding.

Being Resourceful also means knowing what not to focus on, and one thing I see startup founders do a lot is jump over dollars to get to pennies. You definitely need to be frugal in a startup, but obsessing over anything under $100 is likely not worth your time unless you're completely broke.

Worrying about costs under $100 will send you down a rabbit hole of frustration and lost time. You'll spend half the day and all your mental reserves chasing down, arguing, and contesting a $49 charge with the merchant, your credit card company, or bank.

Also, don't be cheap with yourself. It's much better to have the good cup of coffee and decent meal then live like you're in a prison camp. Treat yourself every now and then. Otherwise, what's the point of it all?

One way to value your time more is to know your Effective Hourly Rate (EHR). This is the amount that your time is worth and is based on your income divided by the number of hours you work. Remember it and post it on your computer or the top of your to-do list. If you don't know your income or don't have any, then set it at $100/hour. I'm serious; founder work is easily worth that if you're being effective.

Also for motivation, always remember, "I'm being paid $100/hour for this; this is valuable work." If you have extra time, handle the small stuff, put it on a list to do later, or get a virtual assistant. The best business people pay others to make problems go away.

Superpower #10: Personal Productivity

"He who works all day, has no time to make money."
—John D. Rockefeller

This section may seem a little obsessive on the productivity concept, but please bear with me as I believe it's critical to understand why and how others get things done and why others do not. This ability is absolutely fundamental to business and life.

By developing your Agency and Resourcefulness, you will be far ahead of the curve in productivity. However, there are many things you can do to also dramatically increase your effectiveness. Again, not every great founder does all of these, but they usually employ others that do.

In my opinion, Personal Productivity is made up of the following elements:

1. **Focus**. Also known as prioritization, Focus is making sure you have your one big goal in mind (in this case, it will be the business) and working on the most important next step in

reaching that goal. I recommend only one big goal and never more than three. Productivity is absolutely useless if you don't work on the right things; you'll just be really good at getting the wrong, unnecessary, or unimportant things done.

2. **Sense of urgency.** Some people have great Focus and then the task will sit for weeks on their to-do list with no action. There's not a lot of time to goof around when starting a business or working in a startup, so you need to have a sense of urgency and know that you don't have all the time in the world.

3. **A Deep Work routine and mindset.** If you are ready to get things done but are interrupted a thousand times a day or constantly putting out fires, then you won't get things done or will get them done poorly. The most productive people schedule and treasure their Deep Work, which we'll discuss below.

4. **Productivity tactics and digital fluency.** After you cover the three things above, there are many tactics and digital tools that will dramatically increase your productivity. We go over those later in this chapter.

Focus

"People think focus means saying yes to the thing you've got to focus on. But that's not what it means at all. It means saying no to the hundred other good ideas that there are. You have to pick carefully. I'm actually as proud of the things we haven't done as the things I have done. Innovation is saying 'no' to 1,000 things."
—Steve Jobs

"[Focus] is the one habit I find over and over again that is present in every single successful self-made millionaire I study."
—Lewis Schiff

You can't have Agency without laser focus. From the example about getting $1,000 above: I need to save my loved ones life right now, so I'm totally focused on this one task. I am not going to check email or Facebook right now; I need to focus. Prioritizing is a related concept. A lot of entrepreneurs can be "busy" all day and get nothing important accomplished.

A study was done on wealthy entrepreneurs and focus was by far the #1 thing most of them credited to their success. Yes, you probably have 10 big things you want to do or build, but I guarantee if you try to do all of them you won't get them all done and most will be done poorly.

Focus on one big thing (or at the most a very few big related things) and watch them get done. Steve Jobs was obsessive about this point—we're doing the iPhone this year and nothing else new—so this focus principle even works with huge companies.

Some people are productivity experts at doing completely irrelevant or unimportant things. Their computer desktop or email folders will be completely organized, but they're not working on anything close to their priority. Honestly, working on the priority can be messy sometimes, so an ultra-clean desktop or workspace is not always the indication of productivity (though less clutter helps clear the mind, in my opinion).

Prioritizing can be tricky (everything seems like a priority some days!), but a great question to ask yourself is: "What's the one thing I need to be working on now to move my goal forward?" Many times, just realizing what's a waste of time at this moment is helpful.

For example, here's a list of things that are probably useless before you've reached Step 1 or 2 in this book:

- Long business plans
- Growth plans beyond a few years
- Elaborate emergency plans for a business that hasn't started yet

- HR manuals before your first hire is needed
- High-tech project management software; start with the basics, then grow
- Complex stock ownership scenarios and business entity plans

Most importantly, perhaps, great founders also tend to focus on doing what they are good at and delegating the rest, especially stuff that drains their energy or work they despise. My life changed dramatically when I delegated the mundane and tedious to others (others who may actually like that work).

Prioritize your list of things that need to get done and work it from top to bottom. Take your priorities and pick the most important one. Delegate the rest or at least batch it with other undesirable tasks.

Finally, it's hard to be focused with 15 apps sending you notifications or checking text and emails every 10 minutes. You know this is bad; stop doing it.

Sense of Urgency

> "Every cent of my personal wealth and business's success has infinitely more to do with speed than with perfection. I know how easy it is for worthwhile projects to die in the Doing, so I'm eager to get them Done in a first version, not exactly right, certain to warrant later improvement and get them launched, out the door, into the marketplace."
> —Dan Kennedy

If there's one thing in life that drives me bonkers, it is founders (and employees) who seem to have absolutely no sense of urgency. They move slow, act slow, and are always carefully over-thinking and over-planning. They seem to be of the mindset that they have all the time in the world to get things done and are happy to let the world wait on them to do it.

I'm here to tell you that not only do we *not* have nearly as much time as you think we do in life, we also don't have forever to wait for you to act on your business. Let me put it this way: I've rarely seen a successful entrepreneur who moves slowly. Usually, people are astonished at how quickly entrepreneurs move.

Now, I've known plenty of successful investors, big company CEOs, artists, and more who happily and effectively move slowly and deliberately, but not a successful startup founder or employee. Business simply moves too fast these days, and it's only getting faster. You need to light the fire.

A Deep Work Routine and Mindset

Once you know the priorities of execution, then a way to radically simplify your life is to make your productivity a daily routine. There's a myth that great artists and other creative types need massive inspiration and have no schedule or routine. I've found nothing to be further from the truth. Most have dedicated times when they work and create.

This list may seem long, but in reality, most of it is about learning the basics then building a great routine that you really never have to think about once it becomes a habit. It becomes part of your subconscious. Having a routine is actually a key to having more freedom in life.

All told, I estimate there's less than 1 hour difference in a day between an exceptionally productive person and your average person who doesn't have a routine or skills and gets much less done: 5–10 minutes planning tomorrow, 5–10 minutes reviewing tasks/goals, 20–30 minutes exercising (to create energy and reduce stress), then arranging their day around proper Deep Work.

1. **Health and energy first.** There's a reason why I made this the first founder superpower and a reason why almost every high-performing person I know prioritizes health. It's the source of energy and clarity to get things done in

life. Energy leads to momentum and focus. Don't ignore your health.

2. **Know your chronotype.** Some people are creative and alert first thing in the morning at 6:00 a.m., and some people, like me, have never had a creative thought before 2:00 p.m. and wake up feeling like a hungover zombie. This is your chronotype and it's important that you schedule your important work to match when you can think best *and* when you're at your optimal energy level. If you're a night person doing a morning person routine, then you're going to have a rough time. Learning this was a game-changer for me. Make sure your team and family understand chronotypes as well so that they respect your most productive hours. You *can* change your chronotype, but it's difficult.

3. **Schedule work how you work.** Know your most productive time and put it in your calendar in chunks that let you do real Deep Work. No meetings, calls, emails, etc. during this time. For some people, this may mean splitting up your day: 2 hours admin, 2 hours deep work, 2 hours sales or training, etc. For others like myself, I like to dedicate an entire day (as much of it as possible outside very basic Process Work) to a big task and even a week or month theme to a big project where I try to focus as much as possible on that one thing.

4. **Improve discipline by planning.** Discipline is making the good things easy to do (meal prep for eating right, exercise clothes ready for exercising, etc.) and making the bad things hard to do (no booze, junk food, toxic people, etc.) in your environment.

5. **Habitizing goals.** Taking your goals and turning them into daily routines that are achievable is the source of an enormous amount of progress and success. For example,

daily exercise, daily writing, ten daily business ideas or ten daily cold calls.

6. **Keep your Vision in mind.** You can do all the productivity hacks in the world, but if you don't remember why you're even doing them day to day, then you may lose focus and motivation. Keep the "why" in mind. Something as simple as, "I'm building the next great X" on the top of your to-do list can be very helpful.

7. **Understand and do Deep Work.** Cal Newport's book *Deep Work* shows that in an 8+ hour day, it's not realistic to do more than 4–5 hours of real, thoughtful, valuable mental work where you are "in flow". It can take up to 20 minutes to get into flow. Understanding this and doing Deep Work is the key to not mindlessly overworking for what is ultimately diminishing returns.

8. **Minimize interruptions and distractions**. Because it requires sometimes 20 minutes or more to get into flow and one "Hey, you got a minute" interruption to kill flow, you need to minimize interruptions. Shut down email, and silence your phone (put it out of the room even). Disable all notifications on all devices that are not critical. Respect that your team may need to minimize interruptions as well. Request if they have time for a chat before a full interruption, then you can to go to email or discuss later. Note: Interruptions costs U.S. businesses $588 billion every year. Workers typically waste 28% of their day handling interruptions.

9. **Identify and do Real Work vs. Process Work.** "Process Work" (also known as Admin Work) is the recurring work that needs to get done for your customers but doesn't improve or move the business forward. Make sure you and your staff do "Real Work" (projects that improve the company based on strategy and goals) instead of just Process Work all day—preferably first! Aim for at least

10% Real Work once operational and considerably more during startup. Note that most of your staff will probably think Real Work is Process Work so make sure they know the difference. Just because everyone is busy all day doesn't mean things are moving forward. More on this in Step 5.

10. **Track your time.** If you want to see how much "Real Work" you're actually doing, track your time for a week or two in an app or spreadsheet. Most people are astonished when they methodically track what's actually getting done. Those 60 Hour weeks are usually far shorter when measured in real work and even Process Work. A totally eye-opening experience for me was finding out that I was wasting half my week, mostly with distractions. This will also help you identify your ideal chronotype or the hours that you're most productive.

11. **Focus on 80/20 work.** Closely related to Deep Work is the Pareto Principle (popularized by the book *The 80/20 Principle*) that says that 80% of results are going to come from only 20% of your effort (and this same principle is demonstrated throughout life: 20% of customers usually produce 80% of profits, 20% of criminals cause 80% of crime and so on). This also means the reverse: 80% of your time only accounts for 20% of your results, so it's critical that you identify your 80/20 work and focus on that relentlessly. The key is identifying 80/20 work (Hint: it will likely be Deep Work), and it usually involves things with high payoffs: planning, creating, writing, building, selling, marketing, systemizing, and anything that moves your business forward or helps you create, scale, and market a better product or service to your customer.

12. **Force the work.** Many times, there is some uninteresting and mundane work that needs to get done or you're just having a hard time "getting down to it." (This is something

you'll want to delegate as soon as possible.) You can punch through this by using the Pomodoro Technique or Cycles by Ultraworking, which help you focus on just doing one timed session or cycle of work at a time (20–40 minutes) followed by a short break. It forces you into Deep Work, and I highly recommend it; some people see 40% or more jumps in productivity. Another good mantra is "don't think, just start." The Chapter Resources has links to further details on these methods.

13. **Reading is working**. As you'll see later, almost all "leaders are readers" and reading is important work. Warren Buffett spends much of his work day just reading. Schedule regular time to read and don't feel guilty; reading is real work, even if it's fiction. (I find science fiction gives me great business ideas.) Obviously, there's a balance, and I prefer action, but reading is great as long as you're getting things done.

14. **Use flow and momentum**. Sometimes, you have days or days of the week (for me this is usually a Wednesday or Thursday) where you are really getting into the flow of things and creative juices are just flowing, much how an athlete has bursts of activity. Try to use that momentum and keep going for as long as you can, but quit before you run out of gas so you can save some energy to reignite later. Don't pull all-nighters unless they're necessary.

15. **Say no a lot**. If you spend hours and hours negotiating deals, contracts, or partnerships that don't have great potential, then you're probably wasting time; just pass on them. I think I've lost entire months to phone calls, meetings, and emails about deals that never even came close to materializing. Don't tell everyone to pound sand, but you can say, "Sure, if you can send the details via email, then I can see if it's something I want to discuss later."

16. **Keep your promises**. Nobody likes people that can't show up on time or don't do what they say they will do. If you want to be known as someone with Agency or even respected, you'll respect others' time by keeping your promises.

17. **Remember your Effective Hourly Rate (EHR)**. Discussed earlier, you probably want to put your EHR right at the top of your task list so you know the kinds of things you should spend your time on and the things that are not worth your immediate attention. This same principle applies for hiring. If you can hire someone for less than your EHR to do something that you hate, then that's something to consider. Finally, some hires will make you even more money, so if someone costs $50k/year but makes you $100k/year (a good salesperson for example), then that's a pretty easy decision.

18. **Delegate and elevate**. The book *Traction* by Gino Wickman shows that leaders need to focus on what they're best at, and this includes delegating what they hate or are not good at and focusing on what they *are* good at. You also need to admit when you need help. If you want to magically transform your business, get good at delegating. There's more on this in Step 5.

19. **Keep personal and business separate**. Many founders become one with their business, and this can make you feel like you're always working. Make sure to "clock out" at the end of the day, even if you work at home (literally close the door to your home office). Try to keep your personal communication separate from business. For example, keep a separate phone for business or don't text/email with business contacts on your personal phone.

20. **Purge negativity from your life**. Politics, news, social media, toxic people, interpersonal drama, and more can simply drain your energy. I recommend you cut out anyone

or anything that doesn't give you energy. Note that this includes that friend or employee who is "great", but for some reason seems to just give you grief. They'd probably be better suited somewhere else, and your energy will skyrocket once they're gone. Additionally, sometimes you simply have to fire a client who makes life miserable (and your team will love you for it).

21. **Triage when super busy**. Sometimes, the amount of work is simply overwhelming and this usually comes in bursts. You may have hundreds of emails and tasks; ruthlessly prioritizing by important and urgent is the only way to stay sane. Tip: Set up an email autoresponder that says something like, "I'm in the middle of a huge project right now, so I'm not able to answer emails right away. Please text or call me if it is urgent." Feel free to turn this on whenever you want, even if you just need a breather. Another tip: Sometimes you just need to ignore all communication for a while and trust that people will follow up with you directly if it's urgent. There's more tactics on email later in this chapter.

22. **Do mental reboots**. When your computer gets slow and acts funky, then you know what to do: Reboot it. I believe humans should do the same. I have a specific "reboot protocol" I do whenever things start to get out of control that includes meditating for ten minutes (learning meditation properly is like taking a flamethrower to your "problems"), exercising, taking a hot then cold (contrast) shower, reviewing inspirational pictures, viewing a favorite movie, or just being grateful for what I have. This puts me back in the saddle mentally and prevents me from spiraling into a worse mindset.

23. **Spend money on your development**. It still amazes me that some entrepreneurs will hesitate to spend a few bucks to get the premium version of their favorite software, buy a life-changing book, get a massage, or get the coaching

or training they desperately need. Spend money on your personal development, and don't feel guilty about it. It's a business expense, anyway.

24. **Remember the work is never done.** I used to have anxiety about the massive size of my task or reading lists until one day I realized this was silly and the work will never really be done and that's fine. There's no special reward for completing all your tasks, and any leader or forward-thinking human will always come up with more tasks each day, so what's the point? Just make sure the important things get done.

Productivity Tactics and Digital Fluency

These are massive time-saving tactics that will explode your productivity, especially if you've implemented the above-mentioned items. Adding digital tools to your productivity arsenal can also dramatically simplify your productivity.

1. **Learn the GTD system basics.** *Getting Things Done* by David Allen is by far the most popular personal productivity system amongst entrepreneurs, and there's a reason why; it's an in-depth system that covers many aspects of getting organized and tracking projects and tasks. I recommend the book if you have time or at least one of the excellent summaries online (linked in the Chapter Summary). Here's a bare-bones summary of overall principles to the system with some of my own interpretations:

    a. **Collect and capture to clear your head.** Capture everything into an inbox or task list so you can clear your head. Minimize and try to centralize your various inboxes or collection points: one email inbox (forward all of them to one inbox), one physical inbox (maybe one for remote work or home office), one task list, one note-taking application or notebook.

b. **Inbox Zero**. Process your inboxes (physical and virtual) regularly and try to get to Inbox Zero (zero items left) if your communication stream is capable of it. In the Chapter Resources, I list some apps that can help you with this process by filtering your email.

c. **Correctly process incoming items**. When processing incoming mail/email, etc., touch it once and take action or create a follow-up. You want to make a decision immediately. The average employee spends one month a year re-reading information without taking action—an enormous waste.

   i. Do it: If it takes less than a few minutes, just get it out of the way.

   ii. Delegate it: Forward it to someone that can do it for you.

   iii. Schedule it: Put it on your calendar or on your task list.

   iv. Defer or process later: Sometimes something is not urgent, and you want to read or review it later.

   v. Delete it or archive it: Archive and label anything you want to reference later.

   vi. "Someday/Maybe" and "Waiting For" lists, labels, or folders. These are great for keeping items you may want to do later or items that you're waiting on a response from.

d. **Review regularly**: Have at least a weekly review to process, prioritize, and organize all of the above. This is a critical step to making the system work.

e. **Focus on action**: The purpose of the whole system (that is lost on a lot of people) is to have a clear mind and more consistently take action on your tasks. A lot of people forget this and get lost on the specifics of the system. Review your task list and calendar daily and get the work done—that's the point. Make sure tasks are broken down into simple actionable steps and are not vague like "write a book." Finally, 10–15 tasks a day is probably enough before overwhelm kicks in (and you may need help); I prefer 5–10 or less.

2. **Use a digital task manager.** There are literally hundreds of to-do and task management applications, many of which are GTD-friendly. Choose one you like and that you'll actually use and works well on all of your preferred devices. Make sure it has recurring task capability so you can begin systemizing and delegating your recurring tasks. Consider one that allows your team to collaborate with you in addition to managing your personal tasks, one that easily allows you to delegate to others.

3. **Use a digital calendar.** Even if you're not extremely busy, I believe you should learn how to use a digital calendar effectively. I don't know many successful founders who aren't a calendar ninja. They usually know exactly what they're doing for the next few weeks and can pull it up immediately if they need to schedule something. Get good at scheduling and using proper notifications and reminders.

4. **Maintain routine checklists**. Checklists of weekly, monthly, and quarterly tasks (don't do repeat tasks haphazardly, do them in batches) added to your recurring tasks and calendar. Do this for your company's tasks and your personal tasks as well. This is a big head start on systemizing your business and delegating covered in later steps. There's much more on this in Step 5.

5. **Take good notes and keep lists**. You'll be learning a lot of new stuff so keep good notes. Use a notebook or software you can access from all devices. Again, for simplicity I prefer one electronic document for everything related to your company's operations like the Startups

Made Simple Planner. Trust me, it's way better to get bad notes now then try to salvage them from memory later. Use folders, notebooks, or tags to organize by topic. Advanced notetakers and knowledge workers should definitely consider creating a "commonplace book" or "second brain" for which I have recommendations in the Chapter Resources.

6. **Learn email hacks**. Email is vastly superior in almost every way as a form of communication. It is easily searchable, you can add attachments, cc people, review the conversation, star it, save it, forward it, forward/copy/paste into task software, etc. As said by Naval Ravikant, "Text is precise, compact, indexable, transmissible, translatable, asynchronous and quick to absorb. Intelligent, busy people prefer text."

   a. Check email as few times a day as possible and either reply now (if it takes a few minutes or less) or star for later and archive (label if you want).

   b. Star everything that's not resolved or for which you're waiting on something and archive (to get it out of the inbox).

   c. Once a day, check starred items top to bottom and take action or update anyone who is waiting on you or vice versa.

   d. Be brief, thoughtful, and clear. Use one email thread per topic (nobody likes going through eight different emails on the same subject) with a clear, searchable subject for easy finding later.

   e. Put what action you are looking for in the email (use #s if multiple items). Many times I get emails from people that I have no idea what to do with. Just ask the question or ask for the task to be done. Highlight in red if it's an action item that is buried in a longer email.

- f. Only "Reply to All" if you're adding something everyone needs to know. Keep it as short as possible, add supporting info (links, invoice #s, all relevant info to make a decision), and make sure you are clear (you're either communicating something or asking for something).
- g. If you need to update yourself or add more data, forward the email to yourself with the additional text, attachments, etc.
- h. Create a "Process Later" folder and a recurring calendar reminder to check it regularly. Put everything that you don't want to deal with now or can wait until the next scheduled review. If I know something can wait until my next Weekly Review on Monday, I throw it in that folder. To get to Inbox Zero now, Star important emails from the past few days, select all emails in your inbox and move them to this folder.
- i. Create a "Waiting" folder and a recurring calendar reminder to check it regularly, usually during a Weekly Review.

7. **Get an assistant**. Some people simply cannot, for various reasons, integrate any of these tactics into their own life, have more tasks than one person can do, or may have disorders like ADHD. If that's the case, then I recommend you get an assistant who is familiar with all of the concepts above (have them read this chapter and print out these lists) and let them manage your inbox, calendar and task list. A great assistant can be a game-changer in your effectiveness.

A Sample Day

You can probably gather by the length and depth of this section on productivity that this is one of my personal strengths. I've been informally coaching people on productivity for a while, and one of the things that illustrates this best and others have found helpful is how a sample day works for me.

My Productivity Guidelines:

- Remove the inessential: Unnecessary meetings, low-priority projects and negative people.

- Goals List. I keep a list of goals for myself and the business. The business goals are known by everyone on the team and are prioritized quarterly.

- One big focus: I work best when I have one big project that I focus on until it's complete. Sometimes more, but usually I have one big project that takes the most of my time.

- Automate: Most of my bills are on autopay or come through digitally. If there's a routine or workflow I can easily delegate or automate, then I do.

- Delegate: I've documented and systemized my Process Work and delegated most of it to others, especially work I dislike.

- Meetings: No meetings before 1:00 p.m., and I try to stack them all on one day a week, one after the other. I don't have meetings unless absolutely necessary and especially if a phone call, screen-share, or emails will work.

- Emails: I prefer almost everything in writing for tracking, accountability, and for many other reasons mentioned above. Inbox Zero daily. I despise voicemail, and phone calls usually make me simply have to write things down, which is why I prefer email in the first place. (FYI, several CEOs that have reviewed this book mentioned that this was their favorite bullet-point in the whole book.)

- Momentum: I don't expect the same level of productivity each day and tend to go with momentum when I hit it.

Some days, I'll get a week's worth of work done and other days a lot less.

- Capture: I capture all tasks and ideas immediately using task management or note software on my computer and devices.

- Weekly review: Clear inboxes, review calendar and goals, and set tasks for the week. I pick 1–3 big things to get done that week.

- Monthly/Yearly I review and assess how I'm doing on my goals and prioritize new ones.

My Daily Routine:

- I'm a night owl, so I wake up pretty late, usually without an alarm, open the blinds, and get some sunlight.

- I go into the kitchen and start the coffee/tea machine and take my supplement stack (vitamins). I rarely eat breakfast as it tends to make me sluggish. While coffee or tea is brewing, I go into the bathroom, brush my teeth, and dress for the day.

- I grab my drink and may chat with my family for a bit, then go into my office or home office. Notice that I've not checked email or news at this point. The night before, I've reviewed what I need to get done today, so I already know what the day looks like, more or less, and am prepared to get right to work.

- Check email and team chat. If I'm not working on a big project, then I scan email for important things and clear my inbox. I use an email filtering service so what used to be over 100 emails is usually around 10. If I have time, I clear out the other folders (where the filters have moved unimportant emails).

- I glance at my task list and calendar to review what needs to get done today. Most of these tasks will be Process Work that I haven't deemed necessary to delegate to others, so I get them done first before I do Deep Work later. Also, I find that doing Process Work first builds momentum to go into Deep Work. Some people like to reverse this order (and also check email *after* Deep Work) but this works best for me because my creativity peaks later in the day.

- I have 4 hours on my calendar nearly every business day for Deep Work, typically from 2:00–6:00 p.m. This is where I turn off all distractions, chat programs, etc. and work on my top project and get into flow.

- During Deep Work I take breaks of 5–10 minutes every hour or so. During some breaks, I exercise with kettlebells or bodyweight, right in my office, which will take care of exercise for the day.

- After Deep Work, I go home and spend several hours with my family, have dinner, relax, and read or listen to music. The point of all the other steps and this book in general is to have plenty of time for this.

- Later in the night, I review my task list one last time to make sure things are done and reschedule and re-prioritize tasks if necessary. Sometimes I'll work and clear emails and tasks, but only if I feel like it. I'll review what needs to get done tomorrow so my brain can think about solutions while I sleep.

- If I have time or feel like it, I will do business reading a few nights per week: books (mostly ebooks), articles I've saved in email, or "read later" apps like Instapaper. I'll save ideas, highlights, and articles in my note-taking app (Evernote) so I can find them later.

- Shower, relax, and personal reading or Internet until bedtime. (Sometimes I'll check the news but that's becoming increasingly rare.) I don't really watch TV but may put on a movie.

As you can see, though I've adopted the many skills, habits, and tools in the lists above, the actual routine once you've internalized and learned them is simple and most days are usually never more than 5 or 6 working hours long (up to 4 of those being Deep Work, which I usually enjoy). I don't even have an assistant. The best part is that I get more done now than when I was working 10 or more frazzled, interrupted hours per day before I adopted this workflow (the 80/20 Principle and Deep Work let me get much more done with less work).

Now, my productivity is basically on autopilot, I don't really think about it and things get done, even exercise. Once you've learned your basic routine and internalized these principles, then begin ruthlessly simplifying your day until you only do what you're best at and what you enjoy doing all day. It took me years to figure out this ideal workflow, so I highly recommend you do the same and watch your productivity soar.

Superpower #11: Good Decisions

"Decision-making is everything. In fact, someone who makes decisions right 80% of the time instead of 70% of the time will be valued and compensated in the market hundreds of times more." —Naval Ravikant

It took me many years to understand the power of somebody who makes good decisions. Get good at making decisions and you almost cannot lose in business or in life. I'm dead serious about this, so please pay attention. Think about it; life is just a series of decisions from what to eat, who to associate with, where to go to school, who to marry, who to go into business with, what marketing strategy to use, etc.

If you can make good decisions and consistently get better at that, then you will mostly avoid the landmines and bad choices that have doomed other people and businesses. Good decisions are basically a "cheat code" for life. Venture capitalists also throw piles of cash at people known for good decisions. Even a 5% better record of good decisions has massive exponential returns in business and in life.

So, how do you make good decisions? The obvious and funniest answer is "by making bad decisions," but that's not entirely correct. You make good decisions by *learning* from your bad decisions. A lot of people never learn from their mistakes. You know these types, and they usually live tragic lives. You also need to take the time to learn about and use good decision-making tools. Again I will mention how powerful even an hour or two of simple planning and thinking through decisions can dramatically improve your life.

A lot of people go through life from one bad decision to another, not really thinking they have any control, then blaming anything or anyone but themselves for their outcomes. Most people get their decision skills from their parents, for better or worse.

More and more, we're learning that just avoiding the bad decisions in life (drinking/drugs, bad diet, anger/violence, bad relationships/divorce, excessive debt, not planning, etc.) will easily put you in the top 20% of a number of important metrics like wealth, happiness, longevity, and so on. A lot of decision-making is simply *not* making some big mistakes as I mentioned in the introduction.

Here are some top landmines and bad decisions that have destroyed countless companies, especially in the fragile startup phase:

- Disagreements and arguments amongst founders
- Bad financial planning or running out of cash
- Lack of financial controls in the business
- Ignoring your market or your customers feedback

- Not learning and applying new skills
- Not getting things in writing
- Anger: treating employees, vendors, or customers poorly (leading to lawsuits)
- Ego: not letting something go or going legal for all the wrong reasons (like hurt feelings)
- Not taking care of your health
- Skirting or working on the edges of the law
- Not planning anything (especially exit or succession) and not documenting your business
- Excessive socializing or getting romantically involved with people at the workplace

Making Good Decisions

Let's go over some basics of good decision-making that I've learned and shamelessly stolen from great decision-makers over the years. The best decision-makers use some of these tools as well as intuition built from years of making good decisions. One tends to get better and better as you internalize these principles.

> 1. **Decisiveness**. You don't have much time in business to wait, so you need to place a sense of urgency on making decisions. You'll likely never have 100% of the information you need to make the decision. Jeff Bezos, founder of Amazon.com, says, "Most decisions should probably be made with somewhere around 70% of the information you wish you had. If you wait for 90%, in most cases, you're probably being slow."
>
> 2. **Be conscious and aware of decisions**. A lot of people go through life on autopilot. These decisions include what to eat and how to take care of your body (over the

long term), what to learn, what to focus on, who to marry, who to work with, where to move, and similarly important decisions that can potentially have a big impact on your life. Pay attention.

3. **Be deliberate.** Set aside some dedicated time to actually think through a big decision, collect the information (opinions of others you trust especially) you need, and put things in writing. Writing equals clarity. Sometimes, even thirty minutes of dedicated time can bring about massive clarity. Also, make sure you're relaxed and not under too much stress. Finally, act like you're deciding for a loved one instead of yourself to help take out any biases (e.g.: you may be too easy or too hard on yourself).

4. **Reversible or not**? Jeff Bezos has what he calls Type 1 decisions that are not reversible and you need to take great care in making them. Type 2 decisions can be reversed, so you don't need to overthink them; you can take the plunge and correct course later. It's important not to confuse the two types because it's silly to waste too much time on a Type 2 decision. A Type 1 decision would be completely changing your company's name, products, and services whereas a Type 2 decision would be adding a new product or service. At the least, Type 1 decisions should be tested before jumping in feet first.

5. **Pros and cons.** Everyone is familiar with this tool but most don't really use it. This is a helpful first swipe attempt at making a decision that has many factors. One way is to make a lists of pros and cons, but it seems that even writing out a story or narrative will make you think through the issue in a more complete manner. Sometimes, this alone can make a decision very clear. The author Seymour Schulich likes to take this one step further and assign each pro and con a score from 1–10. Tally the scores and if there are at least twice as many pros as cons, then it's likely something that should be chosen.

6. **Second-Order thinking.** It's amazing to see, but most people don't really think through what will happen after they make their decision. Often, your team won't understand why you're rejecting an otherwise "obvious" action. Good decision makers are always thinking "then what happens?" over and over when contemplating a choice so they can anticipate the effects of their decision. First-order thinking is only thinking about the immediate effects and can miss out on potentially devastating after effects. Try to think out several months or even years ahead. For example, it sounds great that we're going to focus on a new market, but if we do that, what will happen to our existing market, revenue, focus, what will our existing clients think, what will our vendors do, etc.

7. **"Hell yeah! or no."** Serial entrepreneur Derek Sivers recommends this principle, especially if you are already busy or over-committed. Unless it's something that you would say "hell yeah" to, then pass and maintain focus on your existing priorities. The successful entrepreneur Naval Ravikant further clarifies his tough decisions with the rule: "If you can't decide, the answer is no."

8. **Jeff Bezos' regret minimization framework.** Again, Jeff Bezos shows how much effort he puts into decisions with this one: We can never predict the outcome of a decision, but we can severely regret never having tried. Bezos likes to project himself forward in time to 80 years old and see if he may regret missing out on the potential upside of a decision. For example, he thought he would massively regret not trying to open an ecommerce business in the early stages of the Internet.

9. **Choose the more painful choice in the short term.** Naval Ravikant has realized over time that almost all long-term gain comes from short-term pain (exercising, eating better, planning, saving, etc.). So if you have two choices to make and they are relatively equal, then choose

the one with the most short-term pain, and that's likely to have the best long-term gains. Absolutely brilliant.

10. **Think from first principles**. This is an advanced tool, but great entrepreneurs like Elon Musk take decisions a step further and even question the assumptions behind the possible choices. For example, when he knew he needed a cheaper battery to make his electric cars affordable, he didn't simply limit his choice as where to acquire a cheaper battery. Instead, he and his team broke down all of the construction and materials in a battery and found they could actually construct one far better, cheaper, and longer lasting than was currently available. This is taking a problem and thinking in first principles, try to take the assumptions down to the basics and work from there.

11. **Adopt Core Values and Principles**. Written values and principles for yourself (as well as your company) can make many decisions easier. For example, if you've adopted a core value of "Simplicity" and the decision is whether to add a layer of complexity to a service or process, the core value tends to help you decide if that's the correct way to go. I'll go more into this topic in Step 6.

12. **Use a decision journal**. As previously mentioned, learning from your bad decisions is an easy way to prevent a lot of problems. However, a lot of various human biases sneak in and over time they tend to dismiss the failures and exaggerate the successes and the reasoning behind them. Simply keeping track of your big decisions in writing (keep one file for "decisions") and noting how they went later will give you huge insight into how to keep getting better at decisions and prevents your biased brain from deceiving you.

13. **Listen to your gut**. Don't discount the thousands of data points that your subconscious is constantly monitoring and giving you signals about. If someone seems

distrustful, then be aware of that. If you get a bad feeling about a deal or person, then take that into consideration. Our gut has powerful instincts, so don't ignore them. Differentiate between a "bad gut feeling" (something doesn't feel right) and fear (totally normal).

Hopefully, I've conveyed the importance of decisions and how you can keep getting better at them. The simple fact that Jeff Bezos appears so much throughout the list above should demonstrate that the world's richest man (as of this writing) places an enormous value on making good decisions and so should you.

Superpower #12: Problem Solving

"It's not that I'm so smart; it's just that I stay with problems longer." —Albert Einstein

Closely related to Decision Making is the thing that many founders and CEOs are legendary for: Problem Solving. As we go through these superpowers, you can see a pattern that goes from Vision to Execution. As we Execute our Vision we will run into all sorts of decisions, hence the need to learn Good Decisions. However, we will always encounter problems along the way, so Problem Solving is critical to Execution. In fact, all of the Superpowers in this book can be considered one part of Problem Solving because that's typically what an entrepreneur does for a living.

In general, the Problem Solving process is pretty basic, but the skills required can vary depending on the problem.

1. **See the problem**. Believe it or not, I've encountered entrepreneurs that can't even see the problem. Either they don't recognize it or are willingly ignoring it. Sometimes, their staff or customers won't report anything, which is a separate issue to address. See Step 5 for some solutions to that.

2. **Define the problem.** This can be harder than it sounds. For example, is this customer complaint the result of one bad decision or something systemic in how we operate? It's important to get to the source of the issue and properly define it. A great tool to help identify issues is known as 5 Whys. You start by asking Why the problem happened and to each answer you ask Why again up to 5 times. This tends to get you much closer to the root of the problem.

3. **Generate solutions.** Brainstorm solutions to the problem. This may be fairly simple or require specialized knowledge. The more competent brains (who properly understand the problem) you can get working on the solution, the better. Sometimes the solution, believe it or not, is to ignore the problem if it's not worth fixing, can't be fixed, or is too difficult to fix. Good problem solvers know when something is worth using resources to fix.

4. **Implement and follow up.** Implement your solution and make sure it works by following up to make sure the problem is actually solved.

Chapter Resources for Chapter Three:
http://www.startupsmadesimple.com

4
LEADERSHIP

"Effective leadership is not about making speeches or being liked; leadership is defined by results not attributes."
—Peter F. Drucker

What is Leadership?

This topic is challenging for a number of reasons. First, the formal definition of leadership, "the action of leading a group of people or an organization," is pretty obvious but not really useful for our purposes. What we usually mean by Leadership is really *Good* Leadership where somebody leads a group of people or an organization *effectively*.

Further, good leaders get *consistent results* and Leadership is getting other people to Execute effectively on the Vision (and every leader should have a Vision). Almost everything you read about leadership is a tactic of doing that.

But that leads to the issue of how you define "effectively." If there's one thing that's been a constant source of contention since business and other organizations were invented, it's that the business owners, shareholders, management, and employees don't usually agree on what Good Leadership is because it depends on your perspective. (Think unions vs. management.)

Does a shareholder care if the Leader is inspiring, gets their hands dirty, or has empathy (commonly mentioned traits of good leaders)? Employees may love these things, but a shareholder would be wondering why the CEO is cleaning toilets, working on the assembly line, or crying their heart out about their employees' problems instead of executing on the company Vision.

In another example, imagine there is a very laid back and jolly CEO who never really demands much from his staff. There's little accountability, he pays them well above market rate, gives great benefits, and has almost no expectations or demands in regard to how things are run. Now, this company won't last long in my opinion (unless they have some "secret sauce" super-profitable business model), but there are many employees who would absolutely love to have a boss like this and would think the CEO was a great leader because their lives were easy and they like the CEO. It's like the sports team who loves the old, friendly coach who doesn't demand much from the team, but has never come close to winning a championship.

On the other hand, you have dozens of famous military generals who are considered great leaders simply because they won battles and wars. It didn't matter if the troops even remotely liked the general (more likely feared or respected); the fact was that the general won, and that's what matters in war. After hearing that Ulysses Grant (the ultimately victorious Union general in the Civil War) was a drunk, Abraham Lincoln famously offered to send him and his other generals a barrel of their favorite whiskey. Lincoln (and most presidents, I assume) liked people that won and didn't necessarily care about how they did it or if the troops thought their general was cool.

Are Most Great Leaders Jerks?

> "There are no wishy-washy rock stars. No wishy-washy astronauts. No wishy-washy Nobel Prize winners. No wishy-washy CEOs."
> —*Karen Salamansohn,* author of *Ballsy*

As I mentioned in the beginning of this chapter, there's a big disconnect between what people imagine to be a great leader and the actual leaders that get consistent results. The more I research this topic, the more I find that many of the great CEOs you read about every day are actually pretty insufferable and difficult to work with, not quite the inspirational leaders portrayed in the media. Sure, there are examples of friendly, warm types, but I'm finding out a lot of that was only public relations. It seems most of the greats had what most would consider a pretty demanding demeanor or outright personality flaws.

Almost every new bit of information, even when I was specifically looking for information on the kind-hearted CEOs, ultimately showed that these people, again speaking in generalities, are hard-driven and demanding at the least. Many are, counter to stereotypes, extreme micromanagers. My company deals with entrepreneurs all day, and let me say that they can be very challenging because they're usually very demanding by nature.

Here are a few examples, and remember that most of these are founders that started small.

- Jeff Bezos, founder of Amazon.com (these are just a few from the book *The Everything Store* by Brad Stone):

    - "As many of his employees will attest, Bezos is extremely difficult to work for. Despite his famously hearty laugh and cheerful public persona, he is capable of the same kind of acerbic outbursts as Apple's late founder, Steve Jobs, who could terrify any employee who stepped into an elevator with him. Bezos is a micromanager with a limitless spring of new ideas, and he reacts harshly to efforts that don't meet his rigorous standards."

    - "Jeff Bezos fit comfortably into this mold. His manic drive and boldness trumped other conventional leadership ideals, such as building consensus and promoting civility. While he was charming and capable of great humor in public, in private, Bezos could bite an employee's head right off."

- "Bezos was prone to melodramatic temper tantrums that some Amazon employees called, privately, nutters. A colleague failing to meet Bezos's exacting standards would predictably set off a nutter. If an employee did not have the right answers, or tried to bluff the right answer, or took credit for someone else's work, or exhibited a whiff of internal politics, or showed any kind of uncertainty or frailty in the heat of battle, the vessel in Bezos's forehead popped out and his filter fell away. He was capable of both hyperbole and cruelty in these moments, and over the years he delivered some devastating rebukes to employees."

- Steve Jobs, founder of Apple:
  - Fired people in the elevator and fired people in front of other employees on a whim
  - Screamed at underperforming executives and chewed out employees at all levels of the company
  - He threw a fit about the color of the vans at his company NeXT
  - There are stories of him berating reporters, doctors, and others for various reasons
  - He was so demanding and persuasive that people have called his mindset a "reality distortion field" meaning he could basically convince people that anything was possible
  - "Imagine that your boss told you straight to your face that your project is dog shit. Next, imagine that this boss is Steve Jobs. Thats what happened to me when I was working as the principal engineer of iPhone software during Apple's golden years." —Ken Kocienda

- Bill Gates, founder of Microsoft
  - Got into shouting matches with other tech CEOs
  - Has been described as an "office bully"
  - Argued with his co-founder Paul Allen so badly that Paul described it "like being in hell"
  - His successor, Steve Ballmer, was famous for throwing chairs across the room
- Daniel Ek, founder of Spotify, has been described as "patient yet fueled by an internal intensity that can border on ruthlessness."
- Meg Whitman, CEO of eBay, got into a shoving match with a subordinate because she felt she was not prepared properly for an interview by the subordinate.
- Andy Grove, founder of Intel, "was known to be so harsh and intimidating that a subordinate once fainted during a performance review".
- Elon Musk, founder of SolarCity, SpaceX, and Tesla, has been described as "thin-skinned and short-tempered" and that his version of reality is similar to Steve Jobs—completely distorted. He's been quoted as saying "not enough of you are working on Saturdays."

You may be thinking surely this is just a few random CEOs, this is not how most other great leaders operate, right? However, as discussed in the book *Who: The A Method for Hiring* by Geoff Smart and Randy Street, a thorough analysis of 313 CEOs demonstrated that:

"Boards and investors have a tendency to invest in CEOs who demonstrate openness to feedback, possess great listening skills, and treat people with respect. These are executives who have mastered the soft skills. We call them "Lambs" because these CEOs tend to graze in circles, feeding on

the feedback and direction of others. Boards love Lambs because they are so easy to work with, and in fact, in our study Lambs were successful 57 percent of the time."

That's a great success rate, well over 50%! This seems to contradict what we've discussed, but then there's this:

"The second dominant profile that emerged from our analysis was of CEOs who move quickly, act aggressively, work hard, demonstrate persistence, and set high standards and hold people accountable to them. We call these CEOs "Cheetahs" because they are fast and focused. Cheetahs in our study were successful 100 percent of the time. This is not a rounding error. Every single one of them created significant value for their investors."

So I think my point is clear: Some of the most effective founders and CEOs in the world aren't exactly the nicest people, and at the least, are pretty demanding. Again, not an excuse to be a raging jerk, but something to keep in mind if people want to guilt you into changing your ways that have proven to be consistently effective. The key is that you must be effective and deliver results to even think you can get away with outrageous behavior. Also, keep in mind that many people that worked for the above-mentioned CEOs absolutely loved them so a lot of the complaints about these people may include a healthy dose of "sour grapes" or even people who were poor performers.

That said, in modern business, a jerk or someone who is constantly firing people is very unlikely to get consistent results. An egomaniac who can't communicate or make good decisions is unlikely to get consistent results. Someone who has no idea what they're doing doesn't get consistent results. I say "consistent" because anyone can get lucky or bully their way to one accomplishment. But someone who demonstrates leadership does it consistently year after year. They consistently lead their team to achieve the results they aimed for.

Many Entrepreneurs are Not Natural Leaders

> *"If you are a highly charged, hard driving, highly successful entrepreneur, then, quite a bit of the time, you aren't going to be a lot of fun to be around, especially for the thin-skinned. But you should not change. I've come to appreciate that the successful entrepreneur is a unique and delicately balanced combination of dysfunctions, bad habits, and personality defects as well as incredible genius, daring, and drive. You don't want to tinker with that. What works for you works, and you need people around you who can adapt to the strange creature in their midst; you shouldn't be adapting to suit them."*
>
> —Dan Kennedy

Related to the previous topic, I'm just going to come out and say it: A lot of entrepreneurs, including myself, are not great natural leaders, and frankly, can be pretty disagreeable if not outright insufferable. They vastly prefer working on the Vision of the company and working with ideas, products, or customers instead of managing the mundane day-to-day of the business, especially dealing with the management of employees. I want to reiterate that this is not a license to be a jerk (there are a lot of failed jerks out there), just a notice that many entrepreneurs need to be careful when taking leadership because it might be difficult for them because others usually don't think like them and that tends to cause frustration.

The good news is that even the most aloof entrepreneur can learn the basics of leadership, at least until they can hire a "people person" who can take the day-to-day management of the company to the next level. Personally, it took me way too long to pick up the basics, and I still struggle, but after 17 years of consistent profits, growth, and making the INC5000, I've realized that I've reached the limits of my leadership abilities and need to step aside to focus on what I'm good at and hire someone who actually likes running the day-to-day of the business. Great serial entrepreneurs know this and will hand off their startups as soon as they can.

The book *Rocket Fuel* by Gino Wickman goes deeply into this dynamic by separating what he calls Visionaries from Integrators. The Visionary is almost always the entrepreneur who founded the company and typically gets overwhelmed or impatient with the management of the company and dislikes "chasing squirrels" and managing people. An Integrator, on the other hand, absolutely loves managing people: motivating, coaching, and holding them accountable. If this situation sounds familiar to you, then you'll want to look into hiring an Integrator sooner rather than later, certainly before 17 years go by. Some people are both a Visionary and an Integrator but this is extremely rare.

So What is Great Leadership?

For our purposes in a startup, I think we need to consider both perspectives when defining a good leader: the *consistent* desired results they achieve (which is what the owner and shareholders care about) and how effective they are at getting their team to *want* to achieve those results. If the team admires or even likes the leader, than that's even better, but none of those things really matter if you're not getting results (and especially if you go out of business because then nobody has a job). Or to put it simply, we need results, but we need to remember employees are real human beings, and their opinion and motivation should matter if you want to build a great company.

Also, there are so many effective leadership styles that it's important you find your own that works best for you. There's the stereotypical outgoing "people person" leader who can rally the team to a great cause, the general who gives the rousing speech to the troops. Then there's people like myself who realize I'll never be that "people person" but work with what I am good at and try to focus on solving problems, creating clear goals, and removing roadblocks for my team. I think many different styles of leadership can be effective, so don't limit yourself to the stereotypes you see in media or read about in books.

So, where am I going with all of this? I'm defining Leadership so that it is clear and also identifying the Leadership Superpowers so you can effectively learn them. If you struggle with some of them, then you may need to hire someone else to manage and lead your company at some point.

That said, I believe these are the Leadership Superpowers:

- **Superpower #13: Good Communication Skills**
- **Superpower #14: Accountability Mindset**
- **Superpower #15: Team Development and Motivation**
- **Superpower #16: Courage to be Disliked**

Superpower #13: Good Communication Skills

Communication can be seen as a way for you to get results, connect with your team, and make sure everyone is one the same page and rowing in the same direction. Good communication skills are critical to a startup; those who cannot communicate quickly, clearly, simply, and effectively will be at a massive disadvantage. A lot of companies are starting to realize that good communication skills, especially written (which is very important in the age of digital and remote communication), is one of the top indicators of an employee's success. I believe good communication skills are even more important for founders.

Why is communication important? You might have the clearest vision, solution, expectations, or insight in the world, but if you can't communicate that to others (customers, employees, vendors, bankers, etc.) then you can't persuade them to follow you, to understand your point, or why they're even showing up for work everyday.

Also, as your company adds people, the complexity of communication explodes exponentially. The book *Scaling Up* by Verne Harnish discusses this:

> "Think back to when your company was just the founder and an assistant with a plan on the back of a napkin. This start-up situation represents two channels of communication (degrees of complexity), and anyone in a relationship knows that is hard enough. Add a third person (or customer or location or product), and the degree of complexity triples from two to six. Add a fourth, and it quadruples to 24.
>
> Expanding from three to four people grows the team only 33%, yet complexity may increase 400%. And the complexity just keeps growing exponentially. It's why many business owners often long for the day when the company was just them and an assistant selling a single service."

If there's one thing you can expect from a successful CEO (and his or her managers) it's that they focus on a very few things and tend to say the same things over and over. This is not because they're boring or close-minded, it's because they know that they need to repeat these things over and over so they become part of the culture of the company and gets everyone rowing in the same direction, especially as communication gets more complex.

Communicating things like the company vision and goals, the company values, and the best practices over and over is how you get these things in the DNA of everyone working with you, and it's effective. It's why your parents likely said the same things over and over as well and why you can probably quote many of those from memory.

Finally, a good founder will detect when communications are bad or are going badly (perhaps in a confrontation among your team) and step in to improve the situation or call a time-out for consideration at a later time when things are calmer.

Writing Skills

Communication skills, especially reading and writing, are becoming more and more valuable for many reasons. Most of our communication is written, more now than ever, even in text messages and chats. It's also expensive and a huge time waste to have to repeat or clarify yourself and to answer the same questions over and over. If you've ever been on an email thread, chat, or text with someone who just "doesn't get it," you know how frustrating and wasteful this can be.

While it solves many quick issues, try to avoid your instinct to pick up the phone so you can develop your written skills. Improving your writing is usually a simple matter of increasing the volume of your writing. Tell your team to put things in writing so they can clarify their ideas and thinking. Writing is so powerful that writing this book actually greatly clarified and simplified many systems I already had in place. Read that again. I'll provide some helpful information on this in the Chapter Resources.

Persuasion

There are very few founders who would deny that being persuasive is a great skill to have. Every great salesperson is persuasive, and while it's not fair, all things being equal, if there are two people competing, the person with the best persuasion skills will get the contract, the sale, the partnership, or even the date. If you're persuasive, you can probably sell something even before it exists. This is a big part of selling your idea to others, and we'll revisit this in Step 4. People underestimate the power of persuasion, in my opinion.

Style and Tone

Electronic communication and social media have been both a blessing and a curse. While these new ways of quickly communicating and connecting have brought about many great things, one thing that has definitely fallen on the wayside is the subtlety of face-to-face and even phone conversations. Here's an example from Cameron Herold in his book *Double Double*:

"I didn't say you were beautiful."

Now, I have no idea how you read that in your mind but there are an many ways to interpret this text, and it usually depends on the mood of the person reading it. Now, re-read it, but put the emphasis on a different word each time. Example: "I didn't say you **were** beautiful" has a much different vibe than "I didn't say **you** were beautiful".

People will read things in their mood (they may be having a terrible day) and misinterpret even simple sentences, so it's important to review your communications for tone and how they may be perceived. It's not *what* you say; it's *how* you say it.

It still amazes me how short or rude some people communicate these days (even employees); it's killing your chance at getting what you want (for example, a promotion). At the very least, use basic "please" and "thank you" etiquette every time in written communication to make sure nothing is misunderstood. People have been fired or lost friends for less, believe me; style and tone are important.

Finally, you as a founder have to set the example and make sure the communications themselves are not overwhelmingly negative to begin with. For example, if you find out your team is not following a clearly written rule or procedure, there are a couple of ways to inform them:

1. You can do an in-person or phone meeting and rip their heads off. The point will be taken and perhaps will stick, but since there's no written record of it, you can't reference it again, and your team is probably either scared or mad now, making things worse. They were probably so terrified that most of the message was lost. It wasn't written, so

it'll likely be forgotten in a week or two, and there's no record to refer to later.

2. You can do an in-person or phone meeting and be incredibly nice and gracious. The point will be taken and perhaps will stick, but since there's no written record of it, you can't reference it again. Your team may or may not change their behavior, but who cares because you heard one thing and somebody heard something else. Search online for "Yanni vs Laurel" to see what I mean about people hearing different things from the exact same sounds.

3. You can write the team an email or memo that says, "Hey, geniuses, nobody's following the XYZ procedure, and I've told you like ten times about this. Anyone not following procedure going forward will be terminated." The point will be taken, and there's now a nicely written record of you informing everyone (which is good, meaning you can reference it later if the behavior has not changed), but the tone will probably just terrify everyone and likely be counterproductive.

4. You can write the team an email or memo that says, "Team, we're having some issues with the XYZ procedure not being followed, and it's creating problems both for us and our clients. The procedure is attached to this email, and we'll discuss at our next team meeting. Please be prepared for questions." This is a) in writing for accountability b) clear and short, explains why the procedure is important c) puts the responsibility on the employee for reading the procedure d) subtly warns that they had better read it and be prepared because we're discussing it at the next meeting (but does not berate them). That's when the in-person component will be the most well received and effective.

Now, Option 4 above doesn't always work, and that's when a formal written warning and perhaps even anger may be appropriate. The main point is that effective communicators have a clear, direct, but usually friendly style about them, and this seems to get better results overall.

Improving Communication Skills

Everybody has their own particular style or preferred method of communicating, and they all can be made effective. Here's what I've learned are the best ways to improve your communication skills. Note that this is always a work in progress (I've made huge mistakes on this front), and the key is to keep improving. I know some great CEOs who can communicate in one sentence what can take others a paragraph. That's a sign of a great communicator.

1. **Same picture in everyone's head.** If I've learned anything over many years, it's that what you know and how you think can be completely different from what your team knows and thinks. Something might be crystal clear to you, and your employees may even say it's clear to them, but in reality, they have a completely different vision of the concept, idea, project, or task in their head. Knowing this should reinforce how important it is that you make absolutely sure that everyone has the same picture in their head and are talking about the same thing. A good way to do this is to make someone repeat back their interpretation of what is being communicated.

2. **Listen more than you speak.** Founders tend to be fast-moving and many have little patience for too much "conversation over action." Try to overcome this tendency and make sure to listen carefully to people, especially your customers and team. Often, your customers or team won't speak up unless heavily encouraged (especially introverted employees), so always ask for feedback and for any questions they might have.

3. **Keep it short and simple**. The best communicators keep it short and simple for easy understanding by your intended audience, especially in business writing. Remove unnecessary words and information. Don't overwhelm people with information that is not actionable right away.

4. **Focus on clarity**. Ask yourself, "What am I trying to say?" and work from there.

5. **Repetition until it hurts**. Your vision, one-sentence strategy, values, principles, best practices, and goals should all be so familiar to your team that they could repeat it word for word. At Amazon, they call these "Jeffisms" because CEO Jeff Bezos endlessly repeats them.

6. **Watch style and tone**. As discussed earlier, style and tone can be massively misinterpreted and it's important to monitor. Light and friendly is best: thanks, no problem, we'll take care of it, thank you very much, glad to help, sorry, my fault, etc.

7. **Be the example and set expectations**. If you're an effective communicator and use proper style and tone, this will filter through your company. Set expectations: If you don't expect a reply to your emails on weekends, let the team know that. I work best late at night, and everyone knows I don't expect a reply until their working hours. I'll call or text if something is urgent.

8. **Over-communicate at first**. When starting out a new company, a new job, a new idea, or simply implementing a new policy, lean toward over-communicating so you know the message or ideas are received. You can tweak things later based on feedback or intuition, but this is way better than under-communicating. The billion-dollar merchant account company Stripe requires all their employees to CC a group email address for all internal communications so communication is out in the open and searchable.

Employees then learn over time which conversations should be actively monitored or reviewed later.

9. **Write things down.** As we'll go over later, writing things down, especially procedures, policies, and FAQs, is a great skill to acquire. There are a lot of "tele-philes" and "in-person conversation" junkies who love to talk all day or use the phone (usually as a crutch for poor written skills), but if you don't have it written down, there's no accountability, and you'll have to repeat yourself over and over until the end of time. Make your team write things down for accountability, and be suspicious of those who resist this. Even an email can be referenced easily.

10. **Make written things discoverable**. You're not a mind-reader and neither is your team or customers. If you get asked the same question more than a few times, then it's time to put things in writing and post them where they can be easily found. We use an intranet and Google Docs (all searchable) for teams and a thorough, searchable FAQ for our clients on our website. Tip: Have your team set their browsers to an intranet page and post memos, notices, and announcements there instead of email. This keeps announcements "front and center" and unclogs email inboxes.

11. **Systemize to reduce unnecessary communication**. Jeff Bezos said, "Communication is a sign of dysfunction. It means people aren't working together in a close, organic way. We should be trying to figure out a way for teams to communicate less with each other, not more." This may sound counterintuitive, but this is an important point in the world of email, text messages, and constant chat. Too much communication and interruption can massively disrupt workflow and Real Work throughout the organization. It's important to have clear systems and procedures to handle the never-ending flow of basic

questions, clarifications, and expectations of how things work. Writing things down and making them easily discoverable will help reduce the volume of communication and is one reason why they're critical to a well-functioning business.

12. **Use a daily huddle.** You can write things down and be more effective at communication, but this doesn't stop interruptions throughout the day. The daily huddle is a good solution to this problem. It's a quick 5–10 minute team meeting (1 minute per person, do a separate meeting for each team) in the morning for everyone to report what they're working on, and if they're stuck, have questions on their work for the day, etc. Done properly, this should massively reduce interruptions and issues through the day.

13. **Use communication channel best practices.** Not all communication channels are appropriate or ideal for every situation. Learn how your business functions best. Some examples:

    - Chat = Urgent; should last only a few minutes, otherwise the concept is too complex and switch to phones

    - Email = 2–24 hours (not weekends; use phone/text if something requires weekend interruption). If you need a reply sooner or before close of business, ping via chat.

    - Phone = complex thing easier discussed live, but ping somebody or schedule the call, don't just interrupt

    - Urgent/personal to an individual = phone/in-person

    - Urgent to the team = chat via the main or "general" channel

    - Intranet = not urgent but important for all to see and reminders of memos and updates

    - Meetings = In-person or video

14. **Use abbreviations and acronyms.** One way to speed up communication in your organization dramatically is to abbreviate and shorten long or complex concepts and phrases (this especially helps for speeding up written communication). For example, in my company, our customer management system called "Business Entity Management Application" is just BEMA, "Ready to Process" is RTP, "Turnaround Time" is TAT, etc.

15. **Learn persuasion skills.** I've never heard someone say they regret getting basic conversation and sales skills, especially a founder. Basic persuasion and sales skills will serve you well throughout life, and are incredibly easy to learn.

16. **Encourage good communication from your team.** Coach and help your team improve their communication as well. A poor communicator is almost always a poor-performing employee. If you have to repeatedly ask them to communicate something to others or clarify why they didn't communicate something properly, then you probably need to start planning for their replacement.

17. **Manage bad communication.** Inevitably, there will be a fight, argument, or worse that will require your intervention. Make sure to intervene and de-escalate as quickly as possible. Try to resolve things amicably and get to the root of the problem.

18. **Use righteous anger when necessary.** Mostly used as a last resort (and often misused by many as a first resort), and provided you're doing most of the things above, sometimes people are just not getting the point or understanding the importance of something or are overstepping their authority and righteous anger is justified. "This is not our focus right now" may be ignored but "This is not the *fucking* focus right now, drop it" conveys a different level of importance. Used sparingly, it can be effective.

Superpower #14: Accountability Mindset

Leadership should be easy if you have a clear vision and you communicate clearly to your team what needs to get done and it will just get done, right? Wrong. Welcome to human behavior in the 21st century. You would be amazed at how hard this can be in the modern workplace. Business is suffering from an accountability crisis in my opinion. It is sometimes hilarious the extent to which some employees will go to avoid accountability or even making the most simple of decisions and how leaders let them get away with it.

Remember, if your employees are also not owners in the company, there's little motivation for them to work beyond the bare minimum unless they are incentivized in other ways. I would estimate that 80–90% of employees do not like to be held accountable or go beyond the bare minimum. This is not me being mean or pessimistic, it's just the new normal and the reason why the definition of a good leader can be different depending on if you're an owner or employee. Employees often think someone holding them accountable is being a jerk, or at best, too demanding. Ask anyone who manages people for a living, and you will not likely get much disagreement on this.

Most employees don't understand the sometimes existential terror of owning a business, making payroll, the threat of lawsuits, being responsible for the livelihood of others, and the dozens of various other issues business owners go through. A lot of people only want their paycheck and to "clock out" at the end of day and not think about work. (And business owners are certainly jealous of this some days!) There's nothing wrong with this, but we do need to find a good middle-ground between "clocking out" and having basic accountability for the job during working hours. We don't expect them to be responsible for the company, just accountable for their particular job so you can *count* on them to get the job done.

Building an Accountable Team

How do we fix this? Almost every modern book, article, or guru tends to hold the employer responsible for this and recommends all kinds of engagement tools to make people want to do their jobs. I'm sympathetic to this mindset, especially in poorly run companies where you have dysfunctional management, unclear goals, or five different bosses.

However, I'm going to recommend something radical for a startup with limited resources: Hire people with an accountability mindset from the beginning and then build accountability into your company. You don't have the time or resources to prod or beg people to do their jobs and deliver on promises; you need people who can get things done correctly and on time.

1. **Hire for accountability**. If you want people to be accountable, make sure you hire for it. This means putting exactly what needs to get done in the job description along with the standards they will be held to. Mention accountability in the job description, in interviews, and when training. Make it clear this person is accountable for the defined results, and if they do not achieve them, there will be consequences. People who like to be held accountable will usually tell you, and in fact, are eager to demonstrate that.

2. **Define accountability.** Related to the above, it would be insane for you to hold someone accountable for something that is not clear, defined, and measurable. Make sure you've *written* and trained on exactly what you expect, what standards you have, and how you will measure them. For example, if you have a receptionist, describe how visitors are to be greeted (what to say, how quickly you greet someone, etc.) and seated, or how phones are to be answered (what to say, number of rings to pick-up, etc.). You can only blame yourself if you're not clear and haven't defined correct behavior.

3. **Use the language of accountability, and get it in writing.** Vague language gets vague results and confuses. Don't say "get that to me ASAP;" say "I need that by close of business Thursday." Don't say "we should fix this;" say "okay, write me up a one-page summary of this problem and your recommended solutions and have to me by close of business Friday via email." When assigning tasks, make sure you both agree what the final result looks like and it's written down, whether it's a final design or 20 cold calls per day, it needs to be something concrete that you can say: Is this done, yes or no?

4. **Reward accountability.** There's a lot of disagreement on the effectiveness of bonuses, gifts, and "spiffs" to employee motivation and accountability, but I believe they are effective if used properly. If you can reward the staff for work done correctly (no missed deadlines or standards) and especially beyond the standard (for example, great client testimonials), then I think that's one way to help build an accountability mindset in a small business.

5. **Correct lack of accountability.** Nobody likes to punish anyone, and in fact, I think a lot of accountability problems are the leaders' fault for allowing bad behavior to continue; they don't like holding people accountable themselves! As discussed in *The New One Minute Manager* by Ken Blanchard, correction can be as simple as a quick conversation, a written warning, and a well-known, documented "three strikes" rule that means you will likely be terminated if we have to revisit a problem after three times.

6. **Pay and treat them Well.** As we'll discuss more in Step 5, you can't expect to pay bottom dollar and get top-dollar performance. At the minimum, try to provide the many non-compensation benefits I recommend. If you're a complete jerk, then you're going to have a hard time, as we've discussed earlier in this chapter.

7. **Teach the Founder Superpowers**. As mentioned many times, if you can create a founder mindset in your staff with things like Agency, Productivity, Good Decisions, Good Communication Skills, etc. then they will naturally tend to be more accountable because they will start thinking like a founder, which means thinking like a problem solver.

A depressing fact for employees who don't like accountability is that outsourcing and other market pressures are only going to make jobs more competitive, so there will be little room to hire people who can't get the job done. There are literally millions of educated, English-speaking people coming online every year from all over the world, and they're incredibly eager to work. There are now overseas accountants that charge $5/hour online, yes $5/hour, which is one tenth what I used to pay a bookkeeper just a few years ago.

While I don't personally prefer this, in the fragile startup phases, you sometimes need to look overseas for the help you need if you cannot find it or afford it domestically. Personally, I recommend building accountability into your organization, and if you can hire great domestic people, they will outperform the overseas employees, and many times the cultural fit is so much better that it's worth the added expense. Either way, there's little excuse for hiring staff who don't believe in accountability.

Superpower #15: Team Development and Motivation

It should be clear now that a leader needs to produce consistent results by having a Vision, communicating well, and creating an accountability mindset within the company. Next, we want to make sure that we're not doing all the heavy lifting and then start developing our team and making sure they're properly motivated to get the job done. Like the topic of Leadership itself, this topic could cover volumes, but for a small startup, there are some pretty clear things you can do to develop and motivate your team.

Define Your Ideal Leader

Different types of organizations need different types of leaders. For example, a very process-driven and detail-oriented company like mine needs a different person than a creative advertising agency or a football team. Some businesses require different leaders at different *stages* of the business. A certain type of leader may be better in the startup phase, but they may need to pass it to a person better for growth or steady management later.

For example, if I could create one in a lab for my company, my ideal leader would be humble, accountability and process-obsessed, move extremely fast, and be good humored and patient. They'd love improving processes, coaching people, and constantly inspiring them to greater heights of performance. Now that I know what I'm looking for (and maybe even admit that's not me right now), I at least know what I need to work on myself and eventually whom I need to hire, promote, or develop within the company.

Right People in the Right Seat

Made famous by Jim Collins in his book *Good to Great*, we want to make sure the people that we hire are the right person for the job. Sometimes, we'll find a person is terrible at one job but stellar at another, even in the same department. This is why communicating well with your team and accountability are important. If you can be honest with an underperforming employee, they will likely admit that while their current job is not ideal, they'd actually be much better at something else. For example, somebody might be working in customer service but would prefer doing sales or administrative work.

As you get more experience managing people, you'll get better at this, but the important thing to realize is that you should try to hire the right person for the right seat in the first place. This is where it's very important to write clear job descriptions, do thorough interviews, and have clear procedures and training where possible. If people are not in the right seat and simply cannot do any other jobs, then you'll want to move them out of the company as soon as possible because poor-performing or toxic employees tend to cause motivation and other issues with your existing team. See Step 5 for more details on this.

Right Incentives

Incentives can be hard to get right, but in addition to rewarding people for accountability and doing their job correctly, I believe you should pay attention to how you incentivize your team. This can vary dramatically from business to business. It's said that the only thing Warren Buffett micromanages in the many companies he owns is the compensation plan of the CEO; he wants to make sure they're properly incentivized for the right things and performance. You want to be careful what you are incentivizing. If you want long-term, strategic thinking but reward short-term behavior, then you will run into problems.

Some employees want recognition or praise, others want training and advancement, some want plenty of flex time or time off, and some just want cash or a thoughtful gift. As your company develops, you'll tend to find the right incentives for the right people as long as you're looking for them. I believe an incentive program based on the performance of the company is effective for many companies, and I've been paying quarterly bonuses based on profitability since my company has had employees. If the quarter comes up short, but we're meeting specific written strategic goals, I will still pay a bonus.

There's a lot of disagreement on how motivating bonuses really are in a business, so make sure that they are conditional on performance and can be taken away based on poor performance. They're not a bonus if they're expected by everyone for no good reason. Consider individual goals and other Key Performance Indicators" (KPIs) to further clarify what "good performance" means.

Regardless if it's bonuses, parties, time off, catered meals, massages, foosball tables, or whatever, the key is to incentivize the behavior you want and hopefully align your team with the types of incentives they want as much as possible. Google, Facebook, and other businesses that basically have a monopoly (or hundreds of millions of dollars in funding) and have high-demand, high-skill employees will obviously be able to offer more incentives than a cash-strapped startup. See Step 5 for more details on bonus and non-compensation benefits.

Remove Demotivators

Like many other parts of this book, I like to focus on things *not* to do and mistakes to avoid as a great way to prevent most problems. A lot is written about culture in companies these days, and in the case of a small startup, simply not de-motivating and frustrating your staff will get you a long way ahead of the game in developing a competent and motivated team and ultimately in developing a high-performance culture.

- **Toxic management style.** As we discussed in the beginning of this chapter, constant yelling, pessimism, negativity, threatening to fire or demeaning people (especially in front of others), poor communication, and other personality flaws won't get you far. (Only the most super-talented of CEOs get away with it.) Most employees quit because of their boss (and not necessarily the job).

- **Poor treatment of staff.** This includes overworking, not listening to their issues, not acknowledging birthdays, paying late, dirty offices/bathrooms, ridiculous policies (requiring a full suit dress code for call centers, no time off for holidays or grieving, etc.), skimping on supplies or resources around the office, and a hundred other little insults that some employees have to deal with at many poorly run companies. The Golden Rule applies here:

treat the staff how you'd like to be treated if you were an employee.

- **Toxic and poor performing people.** Toxic (mean, deceitful, gossiping, whining, complaining, angry, etc.) people need to go immediately. They're absolute poison to a business and potentially can kill a fragile startup. Never tolerate toxic employees or managers; trust me on this. Underperforming employees should be given the opportunity to improve or move to another seat, but if that doesn't work, they need to go as soon as possible. Having underperforming employees in your company sets a low standard and can actually anger high-performing employees.

- **Problems, hassles, and constraints.** As we'll go over in Step 5 and as mentioned in the Problem Solving superpower, identifying problems along with getting rid of hassles and annoyances that your team encounters is a great way to improve motivation and remove things that drain energy. Ask your team what their hassles are, put them on a list, and work them by priority from top to bottom. Ask the same of your clients, and that will tend to make your product or service better and your employees happier as well. There will always be hassles, just get better at solving or minimizing them.

- **Lack of clarity.** What is the purpose of my job? What is the purpose or vision of the company? What is expected of me every day, and where am I headed? These are questions a lot of employees at startups can't answer (and you may not know right away), so make sure that everyone is clear what they're working toward. Much more on this in Step 5.

We can sum up team development and motivation as: define the ideal leader (so you can become or hire one), hire well, incentivize good behavior, and get rid of things that kill employee motivation. This will get you far ahead of the curve in most startups. In Step 6, we'll go over how you'll eventually want to build a Leadership Team to take over the day-to-day management of your company.

Superpower #16: Courage to be Disliked

> *"A manager is severely handicapped, dangerously vulnerable, and certain to be ineffective if he is an approval seeker, a person who needs to be liked by his subordinates."*
> —Dan Kennedy

> *"It never ceases to amaze me: we all love ourselves more than other people, but care more about their opinion than our own."*
> —Marcus Aurelius

Most people want to be liked, respected, and admired; it's built into our DNA to want these things and get along with our tribe. I wish business was all about camaraderie, good feelings, and dancing around maypoles, but that's simply not how it works a lot the time. The truth is that the most effective leaders, as I've shown, are usually not so nice and may even be actively disliked by their team. If our presidents, generals, CEOs, and other leaders in our society led on the basis of being liked, nothing hard would ever get done, and the organizations would likely fall apart.

In reality, many of the most effective teams actually have quite a bit of argument and disagreement; that's how they arrive at honest solutions. Patrick Collison, the co-founder of Stripe, has mentioned that his Irish heritage and cultural tendency to argue over things constantly is actually a great reason why the culture of Stripe is so successful. They're not afraid to mix it up, and this helps get to the truth of things and build better solutions. This can be upsetting to certain personality types, especially the thin-skinned.

As discussed, the average employee, if you're effective and holding them accountable, may not like you that much. It would be great if they did (and as I recommend, you should hire employees that like to be held accountable), and hopefully you will at least earn their respect, but as discussed earlier, you need to produce consistent results, and that usually means being pretty demanding. You need the courage to be disliked if necessary.

Leaders that want to be liked will be very vulnerable to a host of issues, including the inability to confront problems, a fear of holding people accountable, a lack of assertiveness (they'll get railroaded by aggressive employees under them), and the worst of all (if and when you hire managers yourself), the inability to deal with or report these issues to their superiors because they know it makes them look bad.

I hope you can see how badly problems can spiral out of control under this type of leader. They won't confront problems, they won't hold people accountable, the truth about problems will never come out (perhaps even business-ending problems or vulnerabilities, potential lawsuits, theft, etc.), and their staff may bully, ignore, or actively undermine them. This is a recipe for chaos and a toxic environment.

The Balancing Act of Leadership: Respected But (Maybe) Not Liked

As I've mentioned multiple times (so I hope the message is clear), leadership is not a license to be a jerk, and there's no reason for you to be a jerk to be an effective leader. There are many examples of leaders who are well-liked by their team. The problem is that some people will think you're a jerk merely for holding them accountable or noticing poor performance. This is the main issue of this superpower: You have to be willing to be disliked. But there is a balancing act I've seen great leaders do, and there is a way to be respected not liked. I think being respected, if this is something you desire, can be important so long as the person respecting you is respectable *themselves*.

Habits of Respected Leaders:

- **Be the example**. If you don't hold people accountable and confront problems yourself, how do you expect your team to learn or act?

- **Be calm**. Nobody wants to work for a neurotic or angry busy-body who gets frazzled by every decision. Make relaxation a priority (consider meditation or other relaxation tools), delegate things you dislike doing, and remember what I stated in the Energy Superpower: It's all a game. Speaking or communicating while angry is a huge source of regret for many leaders—don't do it. Wait 24 hours; the other party will be corrected or informed eventually.

- **Be humble**. Being humble can make your personality more tolerable, especially when you're demanding. You can be humble and very effective at the same time. Practice quiet, competent leadership.

- **Be positive**. Positivity is critical. Be the Happy Warrior, which I think is a good combination of ruthlessness in getting things done and keeping things upbeat and motivational. Nobody likes to work for a professional bummer, and negative people at work are absolutely toxic and need to go (especially mean, gossiping, and insubordinate ones).

- **Be honest**. If you are honest with your staff, then most good people will respect that even if the truth hurts. Be careful, too much honesty and revealing of fears can terrify a team, so be strategic with how much honesty you reveal; you don't want to constantly scare the team into thinking the business is doomed.

- **Be assertive**. If you're not assertive, then you'll get bullied, not only by your staff, but by customers, vendors, family members, and life in general. You want to assert that you have a right to be heard and to take the necessary actions you feel are necessary to succeed at whatever you do. Certainly, don't be intimidated by your subordinates.

- **Be solution focused.** Don't take things personally; focus on the problem. Take your ego out of business and team decisions. You want the team to succeed, and sometimes you need to swallow your pride and do or say things you don't want to do for the good of the team and ultimately yourself.

- **Be strategic about hiring.** Don't hire thin-skinned people and especially those who cannot take any criticism whatsoever. Hypersensitive people generally do not belong in a startup. It's important for your team to realize that disagreement is not an argument.

- **Be accepting.** This may be the hardest lesson for many high achievers, but you want to accept that other people can do things differently than you, and sometimes it doesn't look effective at first. Accept that others may have a better way of doing things, and let them show you and teach you.

I believe these tactics and the other superpowers mentioned in this chapter will help you become a dramatically more effective leader. As we've seen, Leadership is many times not about being nice or inspiring but is mostly about vision, getting results, and a good honest rapport going with your team. The Leadership Superpower, in my opinion, is easily the hardest to master, so don't fault yourself if you start with very few abilities. As I've mentioned, I struggle with Leadership myself, even after 17 years. You, like me, may realize you may be better served by hiring great leaders and focusing on your other superpowers.

Chapter Resources for Chapter Four:
http://www.startupsmadesimple.com

PART TWO

The 6-Step System

5
STEP ONE: IMAGINE IT

"The essential principle of business—of occupation in the world—is this: figure out some way in which you get paid for playing." —Alan Watts

Imagine the perfect business for you where you are doing what you love. What would that look like, and what would you do (or not do) on a daily basis? Having this vision is the first crucial step in creating your ideal business and is why I consider it one of the founder superpowers.

Why is having vision important? Because there is something magical about the human mind and its ability to make a clear vision a reality, sometimes without you knowing it. Anyone who has built something from an idea in their head knows this; whether it's a business, a dream house, or anything else.

Some of you more scientific types may have flinched when I wrote "magical" above, but fear not, I have science on my side. Having a clear vision in your head activates certain parts of your brain. One of those is known as the reticular activating system or RAS, and its purpose is to filter out unnecessary information and then focus on information that you've deemed important.

An example of this is when you can filter out all the voices and background music in a restaurant to focus on one person. Or, when you have been thinking about buying a particular make and model of a car, you begin seeing it all around town or online. This is your RAS in action.

A similar phenomenon is actually one of a human's cognitive biases called selection bias. You think there is more of something simply because you notice it more. But unlike most biases, which are usually negative, we can use selection bias and our RAS to begin focusing on the things that are going to make our vision a reality.

We're going to make our Vision so clear that your brain will have no choice but to immediately begin working overtime (especially at night while you sleep or doing unrelated activities like walking) to solve the problem you're working on or idea you're thinking about. This is another aspect of our brain called the default mode network (DMN) that works while you are *not* focused on a specific task.

For years, I've been letting my unconscious mind work on problems for a few days and the solutions just come, usually while I'm in the shower, walking, or doing something not directly related to work. Does this sound familiar? Having ideas in the shower or while walking or driving is almost a proverb at this point. This is your DMN, and it works best (mostly by making connections in your brain) when you're relaxed and not focused on something specific.

You'll begin to notice things that will make your idea a reality, suddenly see the clear solution, run into people that can help, or see opportunities and connections that you previously ignored. This is the power of having a clear vision.

Motivation and Desire

We know that if we have a clear vision, our brain will help us make it a reality. This means the next step is to ask yourself what you really want. What is your primary motivation for starting a business? This question seems obvious, but I see many people get this wrong and say things like "to be a millionaire" or "to buy my dream house and car" or "to not be broke anymore."

What I want you to do is take what you want a level higher and really determine why you want to start a business. If you're honest with yourself, you probably want some or all of these things:

- Freedom
    - Financial: freedom from worrying about money ever again or enough money to fund your lifestyle
    - Schedule: freedom to do what you want when you want
    - Control: freedom from having a boss

- Contribution
    - Making your community a better place
    - Helping people with their problems
    - Saving the planet or moving humanity forward
    - Living heroically with purpose and meaning, living with core values and principles

- Admiration
    - Self-respect: to challenge yourself to do something difficult
    - Respect of family, friends, peers, and other important people

- Attraction: to attract the kind of people (or even a husband/wife) who may also have my same values or passion about my chosen industry

- Power
  - To more effectively influence the future or other powerful people

The list above is not exhaustive, but I hope you can see how identifying a deeper purpose to your business can actually make it more powerful when you visualize what you ultimately want in a business. This is powerful motivation, so take the time to do this. It shouldn't take long because it's usually pretty clear when presented like this.

The next step is to turn this motivation into a burning desire. The entrepreneurs who seem to make it are those whose level of desire for freedom (for example) is so powerfully overwhelming that they'll do absolutely anything to make it succeed. This is related to Agency, which we discussed in The Founder Superpowers.

For example, working for others, before I started my company, was so frustrating and soul-crushing for me that there was no way I was not going to have my own business eventually. Anyone who knew me at that point knew I was going to do my own thing before long because I wouldn't shut up about it. I made my freedom a burning desire, and I did absolutely everything within my power (which, admittedly, was very little at that time) to make that a reality.

The Perfect Business

"If just you keep your mind resting against the subject in a friendly but persistent way, sooner or later you will get a reward from your unconscious." —John Cleese

MATT KNEE

Now that we're getting clear about why we want to start our business, it's time to start getting more specific. Remember, we want a clear Vision so we can get our mind working on making it a reality. Even if you have no idea which business idea you will eventually pursue, you probably know the types of things that you are good at, the working environment you prefer, a daily routine, and more.

In the introduction to this book, I wrote about imagining the perfect business for you. This is important because so many entrepreneurs end up trapped in a business they don't like running, a daily routine that is not for them, and having a lifestyle that is not ideal for them. There are so many ways to be successful in business that it's important not to limit yourself to the concept of a business that may not be perfect for you.

Some people dream of owning a huge, world-changing, international company and others simply want a small profitable local business. Some people like early morning meetings and daily interaction with a large management team, and others would prefer a business that pretty much runs itself or can be run from anywhere. It's important to figure out what the size and complexity of your perfect business is before you start it.

Because one of my primary motivations is freedom, I've structured my business so that it doesn't require constant supervision, doesn't require many meetings, and doesn't require me to have a set schedule at all. Frankly, the corporate life is repulsive to me, and I prefer to work from home most of the time with my family. Somebody who wants to build skyscrapers or land on Mars would obviously have a much more rigorous daily routine.

Answer the four big questions about your perfect business:

1. What does your perfect business look like?

    – How big is it?

        i. Successful one-person company

        ii. Small boutique or micro-business (2–5 employees)

        iii. Small business (5–20 employees)

      iv. Medium to large business (20–200 employees)

      v. Major company (500+ employees)

      vi. Franchised or multiple location business (any number of employees)

- Who do you work with? Consumers? Other businesses?
- How many people are working for you?
- What does the office (or retail space, etc.) look like?
- What colors and designs do you see?
- What do others think of your business?

2. What is your perfect day?
   - What time do you wake up and what is your routine?
   - Do you work from home or at the location?
   - Do you work at all or only when you want? Are you free to go on vacation whenever you want?
   - Do you interact with a lot of people, customers, and employees—or not?
   - What do you do at night?

3. How much money do you make per year?

4. What is the endgame?
   - Do you run it yourself and work until you retire or die?
   - Do you keep it in the family after you retire or die?
   - Do you sell it? In how many years?
   - Do you systemize it and hire others to manage it so it keeps generating passive income indefinitely?
   - Do you get venture capital or equity investors to take the company to the next level?

You get my point here. The more you know what is perfect for you, the more clear your vision and the sooner we can start limiting the types of business ideas that would be perfect for your personality and preferences. The endgame is also important as it shows what the priority is for how you set up your company.

The Business Idea

"All children are born geniuses, and we spend the first six years of their lives degeniusing them."
—R. Buckminster Fuller

By imagining your perfect business, you've immediately begun to clarify the types of business ideas that may or may not be ideal for you. If you already have an idea, we'll go over ways to clarify that idea as well.

For example, if you value freedom and imagine working from home with plenty of free time and vacations, you probably aren't thinking of starting a restaurant. Sure, you can start one and *eventually* get to that point of freedom, but if you're bootstrapping and have limited funding, a restaurant is going to take considerable time and money at first.

To begin, let's expose the myths that business ideas are "lightning strike" inspirations and that only certain people are good at generating business ideas (or ideas in general). These myths are pervasive and almost exactly wrong.

First, there are very few ideas that survived intact after launch. Many businesses started with one idea and pivoted to another idea. Microsoft didn't start out selling operating systems, for example. The chat application Slack started out as an internal company tool. There are many examples like this, and the obvious idea was usually not that obvious until the company started getting customer feedback.

Ideas are a starting point, and many times, entrepreneurs play with them for months or years before they even realize the idea could be a business. Many side projects have turned into successful businesses this way. The entrepreneur didn't even know they were an entrepreneur; they were just tinkering with something they loved.

Second, generating ideas and tinkering around with things you like is a natural function and a skill that can be relearned. Almost every human started out curious, making connections, being creative, and coming up with new thoughts and ideas. Do you know a toddler who isn't curious about things? If anything, kids will drive you crazy with questions, ideas, and their creative messes everywhere.

Only something as silly as our current schooling system (based on an 19th century model that specializes in producing factory workers) could take that natural curiosity and browbeat it out of a kid. Schooling mostly teaches you not to think creatively and only to do what you're told. Don't question things, sit still, read these books, do these exercises, etc.

The Perfect Idea for You

It's time to get more specific about the kind of business idea that would be perfect for you. The Japanese have a concept known as ikigai which means "reason for being" or "reason to jump out of bed each morning." Think about it, there's a cross-section of things that would make something absolutely perfect for you to do each day and want to "jump out of bed," and it's likely a cross-section of:

- What you like to do
- What you are good at
- What's needed
- What you can be paid for

What You Like to Do

You want to start with business ideas based on things you like to do. This should be obvious, so I'll just say that if there's one thing you should avoid it is starting a business doing things you don't like to do. Now, you're always going to have to do things you don't like to do in any business, but for the purpose of business ideas, make sure you're at least interested in the industry or topic.

Notice I didn't say "What you *love* to do." Passion in business, in my opinion, is overrated as a starting point. If you're going to wait to start a business you're totally passionate about, then that might be an extremely high bar, though I admire it if you can find it. I believe a true passion often develops *after* you become an expert in something.

Some things to think about are what you would do if you were already a billionaire and had total freedom. What types of projects would you engage in, or what would you like to do daily? A big myth is that satisfaction comes from the money in a business, but there are plenty of miserable millionaires. It's important to identify what you truly like to do.

What You Are Good At

You may love something deeply, but if you're no good at it, then you either need to upgrade your skills or focus on something else or another aspect of that business. Notice I didn't write "What you're an *expert* at." When you explore potential business ideas, you will know if the basic skills required for that business are something you *might* be good at.

For example, I'm very interested in Bitcoin and the cryptocurrency industry at the moment, but my math and programming skills are lacking. Now, this doesn't immediately disqualify the idea in my head; I just know that to get involved at the technical expert level it would probably take a year or two of learning to catch up.

However, and this is important, if I feel that eventually I will get there, what I can do in the meantime is learn everything I can, start a blog or email list on cryptocurrency, meet other cryptocurrency experts, follow the industry closer, follow or hang around other startups and gradually become an expert.

Here's one thing that people miss out on a lot: They're so good at that particular thing that they don't even think it's special or that people would pay for it. Seriously, there's a lot of hidden talent in the world, and it's important for you to identify the low-hanging fruit right in front of your face. Do people constantly ask you for help or advice on a topic? That might be something you are fantastic at but may not realize yourself. It's important to pay attention to this.

Another way to look at it is to identify the Founder Superpowers in Part One that you're already good at, and see if you can apply those skills to what you like to do. For example, if you're already great at productivity, then you can apply that to an enormous amount of businesses or industries. I don't know one industry that is not looking to improve productivity.

You can even focus on that superpower alone and teach it to others: productivity consulting, blog/newsletter, ebooks, training, or just become the "productivity expert" for the bookkeeping industry or whatever your primary interest is. The same thing applies to communication skills, decision making, etc. This is why I call them superpowers; they are applicable and give you skills in almost any industry or business idea.

What's Needed

Many people know what they like to do and what they're good at. However, the other two parts of ikigai are the critical pieces of the puzzle: what's needed and what you can be paid for. If businesses fail for any reason, it's mostly a lack of these two things.

You may be an expert on World War I flamethrowers or at restoring Atari 2600s from the 1980s, but that doesn't mean that those things are necessarily in demand by that many people. "What's needed" is another way of saying "Is there a demand for this product or service?" Do a large amount of people need this enough to make a real business?

Now, there's a famous quote from Henry Ford: "If I had asked people what they wanted, they would have said faster horses" which is hilarious but something I want to clarify. Yes, most people don't know what they want, but identifying "what's needed" is about making sure that you've thought about the problem properly. In this case, people knew that riding horses was way too slow, and they had a strong desire to move faster.

What's needed is to move faster, not a faster horse. This is an important distinction, so you should think about the core problem that people have (wanting to move faster), not necessarily the specific one (faster horse). For McDonald's, it's not about having a better burger (almost every decent restaurant does), it's about having a fast, convenient, and predictable eating experience at every McDonald's worldwide. They didn't solve the "better burger" problem, they solved the convenience and trust problem.

If one of your primary motivations is to help others, a great way to think about business ideas is to frame it as "How can I help the most people possible with my product or service?" This will make you start thinking big about the worldwide demand for your product or service.

Finally, if you can focus on being the best (again, assuming this is needed), then the best product or service rarely loses and usually demands the highest prices, so that's one way to pursue an idea: be the absolute best in the world at it.

What You Can Be Paid For

Back to World War I flamethrowers and Atari 2600s—you want to make sure there are enough people that want to actually pay you to justify your business. Later, we'll go over how to test your idea, and that's why testing and feedback is so important.

For now, it's important to get feedback on your idea from real people. One thing I like to tell entrepreneurs is *not* to keep your idea secret. I know that you might be terrified of people stealing your idea, but one thing to understand is that likely (not always) the idea is not that new. Don't take offense by this, there are very few new things in this world if you really take the time to think about it. Almost everything is a modification or combination of old ideas. For, example, Facebook = People Directory + Photos + Email.

Venture capitalists typically refuse to sign a "non-disclosure agreement" (NDA) with entrepreneurs for even the most "top secret" ideas because they've found that it's actually more of a hassle to sign the NDA then it is to read the idea. Put that in perspective: A VC actually values the time it takes to sign an NDA (minutes) over the vast majority of business ideas.

Ideas, for the most part, are worthless without execution (why I consider execution a critical Superpower). Besides, 99.999% of the world is not interested in your idea now like you are, nor will they likely have the passion you do to implement it, so it's usually pretty safe to share it.

Where I'm going with this, and what we'll go over in Step 2 in more detail, is that it's important for you to contact potential buyers and then survey or ask them if they would pay for your product or service. Ask real customers, and if they're excited and basically react by basically saying "Shut up and take my money!" then you know you may have a winner. You may even find out people are willing to pay handsomely for WWI flamethrowers or Atari 2600s.

How to Generate Business Ideas

As discussed, there are no magical formulas or "a-ha" moments for the vast majority of business ideas. It's mostly a matter of consciously paying attention to your surroundings and developing the skill of generating ideas. Yes, generating business ideas is a skill that can be learned. Here are some of the principles that have proven to be true among the greatest "idea people" in history.

Principles for Generating Ideas

1. **Be on the hunt for ideas but be patient.** Remember when we discussed the RAS earlier? For it to work, it needs to know what to focus on. Have your vision of your

ideal business in your head, and specifically command yourself to utilize these other principles. You've now told your brain to be in problem-solving mode, and that's the key to finding ideas. Be patient and focus on becoming a person that has startup ideas, and the ideas will come. Chance will favor the prepared mind.

2. **Identify what you are already good at.** This is where an electrician or chef will start their own business based on their existing skills. This is how the majority of businesses are started, so it's usually fairly obvious but we want to put this through our ikigai framework above to see if this really is our perfect business. Also, make sure to identify business ideas you may not be aware of. Are people constantly asking you for advice on a certain subject? Ask some friends to tell you what advice they go to you for. Which of the superpowers in Part One of this book could you apply to what you're already good at? The Mexican restaurant chain Roberto's started when Roberto, the founder, started selling his wife's delicious tortillas at his construction job.

3. **Have lots of ideas and write them down**. One thing not well known is how many failures Thomas Edison had, which was literally thousands of ideas that didn't pan out. Einstein had many scientific theories and papers that went nowhere. It's starting to become clear that being good at having ideas actually means just having lots and lots of ideas, writing them down (you *will* forget; writing = clarity), then ruthlessly trimming the bad ideas and keeping the good ideas for testing. Commit to generating 5 or 10 new ideas a day (no matter how silly), and you'll get better at this over time. Write them down and keep them in the same place so you can review all of them. I use one document to organize mine.

4. **PITA Factor**. One thing great entrepreneurs are good at is identifying the "pain in the ass" (PITA) with everything

around them. They can always see a way to do something faster, cheaper, better, easier, and especially how to make a problem go away. Pay attention to things that drive you (and your friends and family) crazy or things that "should be fixed already;" there are great business ideas in there. The product known as Spanx, created by Sara Blakely, are just pantyhose with the feet cut out (which used to drive her and many other women crazy). Spanx is now a billion-dollar company.

5. **Build for yourself.** Closely related to the PITA Factor is building something you yourself desperately need or want; especially if what exists is lacking in some way. The list of huge companies that come from this principle alone is astounding (Apple, Facebook, Google, etc.). There's nobody more motivated than an entrepreneur who's passionate about their own product or service.

6. **Simplify.** A lot of great ideas are really an old idea just simplified and made easier. You can take something that is currently complex and ask, "What would this look like if it were easy?"

7. **Think big but start small**. Thinking big is a great way to get motivated. However, it can be overwhelming in the idea phase, so choose the absolutely smallest part of that vision that you can test and implement now. The faster you get executing, building your skills, and getting real world feedback, the greater the likelihood of building momentum and success.

8. **Don't obsess about originality**. As discussed, there are very few real new ideas. Are you using MySpace or Facebook? AltaVista or Google? Woolworths or Walmart? Being the first of anything usually makes someone a target or they create the idea that others execute on better. It's not so important to be the first in any business idea and

coming later gives you a head start—there's already a proven market!.

- *"Most everything I've done I've copied from somebody else."* —Sam Walton

- *"Good artists copy great artists steal."* —Pablo Picasso

- *"We have always been shameless about stealing great ideas."* —Steve Jobs

9. **Change your environment and relax**. Most people don't think well in their office or even in their living room, and your RAS seems to make connections specifically when you're not working. They tend to have their big thoughts exercising, showering, driving, walking in nature, and all over the place. This is why a lot of office brainstorming sessions don't pan out; forcing creativity is almost exactly backward. This is also why it's important to keep a digital or paper notebook with you at all times.

10. **Think off the radar**. So many startups these days want to compete directly with Facebook or Google, which is an incredibly high bar. Do you really want to compete with hyper-competitive Silicon Valley? There are thousands of millionaires in industries like zippers, junkyards, small manufacturing, shoelaces, recycling, and hundreds more. Don't just limit yourself to what you see in the business news everyday. The great thing is that competition will usually be much lower in these industries *because* they're off the radar. All the Founder Superpowers apply to almost every industry in the world.

11. **Pay attention to trends**. Anyone can see that drones, 3D printing, and virtual reality (VR) will be big. But you don't necessarily have to be an expert in VR to anticipate what a large VR market looks like (how to treat VR addiction, VR headset organizer, VR productivity consultant, etc.)

12. **Be contrarian**. Go the opposite way of the trend. For example, if everyone is into VR, this means real life experiences are actually *more* valuable now. People will want to see how a farm works, how to ride a real horse, or how to stitch instead of 3D printing. People will want real food, real coffee, and real experiences.

13. **Consider a niche**. Many markets are large and already dominated by big players. However, you can focus on a niche and dominate that small segment. For example, there are lots of yoga studios, but you might open one that's for older folks or men or women or people who do spiritual meditation or different themes/music or combined with weights or diet counseling, etc.

14. **Get 1,000 true fans**. Similar to a niche, Kevin Kelly popularized this concept for artists and craftspeople-entrepreneurs. If you can get 1,000 or more people to pay you $100 on a regular basis, then that's $100,000 each time (or much more, potentially) to get paid to do what you love.

15. **Try brainstorming tools**. SCAMPER is a brainstorming tool (used by Disney and others) that can help you ask questions to generate ideas (or improve existing ones). It stands for Substitute, Combine, Adapt, Modify, Put to another Use, Eliminate, Reverse. You ask a question and generate as many ideas as possible. For example, using Combine, you could take your idea and ask ways to combine it with others. For Eliminate, you ask what you can get rid of to simplify this or take something down to its bare minimum. There are many similar tools and examples online.

16. **Don't analyze ideas immediately**. Once you start generating ideas and that becomes a habit, don't start analyzing them and their feasibility immediately. Go with the flow and just keep generating ideas, and write them down. There will be plenty of time to deeply analyze and test

them later (and we'll go over that), but that uses a different process in the brain—so when you're being creative, just be creative.

17. **Watch/read business biographies and science fiction.** Nothing quite gets the business ideas flowing (and what I call "motivational jealousy") like seeing how a lowly entrepreneur like John Rockefeller or Ray Kroc started from humble beginnings to take on the world. The same concept applies for science fiction as it will make you think of how things might be in the future or how you might want things in the future.

18. **Hustle first.** Consider selling things on Ebay, Amazon, or Craigslist, or become an affiliate or reseller of other companies products/services—or even do random work for pay, especially if you're hesitant to take the full plunge. Many entrepreneurs started out this way, believe it or not; they just fell into a business, and it grew from there. Try to get into something close to what you want to do. This is how you got those Founder Superpowers, get good at hustling and getting things done.

19. **Buy somebody else's idea or business.** Sometimes you don't have the desire or resources to come up with a business idea or perhaps your skills are more on the operational or marketing side of business. The Internet is full of places where you can buy existing businesses, websites, and even pre-made brand ideas. I list some in the Chapter Resources. You can then use the rest of this book to optimize and improve that existing business, and, in many cases, they may have already done the heavy lifting of forming the company, getting clients, etc.

The list above is not exhaustive, but I think it covers the major ways that ideas are generated and gives you a great framework for thinking about your own. Again, I want to emphasize that it's important that you start thinking like somebody that has business ideas and that this may take time. Don't limit yourself, and trust in your brain to work on the problem you've assigned it: creating the perfect business idea.

Signs of a Winning Idea

Everyone is different, and sometimes there isn't much evidence of one idea being better than another until you get feedback. But there are some similarities between winning ideas shared by many great inventors and entrepreneurs. Here are a few:

- **Gut feeling or excited**. It makes you excited or gives you tingles and you can see yourself dedicating a few years to making it real. As discussed, passionate entrepreneurs tend to win.

- **Excited potential customers**. People who may be your ideal customer are excited about it. If they're willing to pay right away, even better. Sometimes this is even called "customer financing."

- **Huge market or potential market**. The five-year outlook is enormous (like VR, 3D printing, cryptocurrency, etc.). It's hard to lose in a huge market that's not saturated yet (but then we can still think about niches in that market), especially an emerging market.

- **High margins**. With some notable exceptions, high-margin businesses are usually better all around. High margins can come from a product or service that is many times better than competitors, highly complex, from a "first-mover" advantage, unique business model, or technology (usually a fast-scaling model), etc.

- **Lowers prices.** Making something cheaper that is currently too expensive.

- **Raises human status.** There's so much cheap coffee and beer available that it actually became cool to pay a lot more for these things. Find a commodity for which people would pay a lot more for a "premium" version.

- **Much better product or service.** Making something much faster that is currently slow. Make something very simple that is currently complex, etc.

- **Recurring revenue and sticky.** Anything where you can get a customer once and continue to have them pay you on a recurring basis is a fantastic business model. It makes your income much more predictable and stable over time. This same idea is "sticky" if it's difficult for the customer to switch to another service or you have no or few competitors.

- **Protectable.** As discussed, most ideas are not new. However, if you have a truly new invention or technology, it's important that you protect it with a patent.

- **Viral or network effects.** Can it be easily spread by your customers to other customers? Think about how Facebook invites your address book or those funny Dollar Shave Club videos shared millions of times.

Next Steps

Step 1 is about focusing just on the idea and your imagination. I've created what I call the Business Idea Generator (BIG) which you can download in the Chapter Resources. I don't want you to interrupt the creative process to move on to more practical things, so continue to use the BIG until you feel like you have a pretty good idea on your hands and are ready to get down to the nitty-gritty.

When you're ready, move on to Step 2 where you'll do a quick business plan so you can test this idea, see if there's a market for it, and begin organizing your perfect business.

Onward!

**Visit http://www.startupsmadesimple.com
for Chapter 5 Resources and to download the
Startups Made Simple Business Idea Generator (BIG).**

6
STEP TWO: PLAN IT

"Plans are useless, but planning is indispensable."
—Dwight D. Eisenhower

"Give me six hours to chop down a tree, and I will spend the first four sharpening the axe." —*Abraham Lincoln*

The only thing worse than over-planning is not planning at all. Yes, I'm going to mention again the importance of even simple planning until I'm blue in the face. Planning is how the modern world was built. One doesn't just throw together a skyscraper or microprocessor (though their first versions were much simpler).

I get a lot of pushback on this step. People either say the idea can't be tested yet, or they're so confident it will work that they think this is a waste of time. For example, I built some productivity software that people loved when I had some basic mockups designed. But we found out during development that mostly people wanted features that were easily copied by the big competitors, and I didn't have the resources to compete with them. Instead of wasting tens of thousands of dollars (and a year or more), I only spent a few thousand and learned some valuable lessons.

I'll admit I didn't have much of a clue what I was really doing with my business before I started writing things down to organize my thoughts. Great ideas became apparent, ridiculous ideas exposed themselves (and were dismissed), and my vision became crystal clear over time. Remember that having a clear vision is a Founder Superpower and key to Step 1.

However, a big problem I've noticed in the past few years is the rise of the "wantrepreneur," someone who knows all about startups, follows Elon Musk and other entrepreneur superstars on Twitter, goes to conferences, watches all the YouTube speeches, listens to all the podcasts, but never seems to actually start a business or even test an idea. This is why execution is one of the most valuable Founder Superpowers; you need to execute on your ideas, at least with a test.

Planning is very important, but it seems the entrepreneurs I've known do either excessive planning (and never get off the ground) or no planning at all (and make critical mistakes), so it's important that we find a better middle ground. As I mentioned in the introduction, most people spend more time planning their wedding than their business or lives. Spend a few hours of planning now to save hundreds of hours later or the unnecessary grief of pursuing a bad idea.

In this chapter, I'll introduce you to the Startups Made Simple Business Plan so you can quickly refine, test, and get feedback on your idea before you waste precious resources on going full speed into launching your business. Our principle will be that a quick plan violently executed (to paraphrase Patton) is ideal for most businesses that are not overly complex or don't require sophisticated science or engineering (like pharmaceuticals, processors, etc.).

MATT KNEE

Beware Professional Bummers

"Keep away from people who try to belittle your ambitions. Small people always do that, but the really great make you feel that you, too, can become great."
— *Mark Twain*

If there's something consistent about people who have business ideas, it's that there will be no shortage of people who tell you it can't be done. The list of things that "couldn't be done" that are now a part of our daily lives is so staggering it would probably take the rest of this book to list it.

Avoid people who never seem to like any new idea. Yes, it's critical that you get honest feedback, but you know the type of person I'm talking about—they've never liked anything new or innovative in their lives, have probably never taken any kind of risk, and generally are what I like to call a "professional bummer."

Let me put it like this: I'm certain there's a professional bummer who could shoot down every idea Elon Musk had and make it seem dumb. They know the business failure statistics and will shove them down your throat. Some people are simply very risk averse, and they aren't cut out for doing risky things like starting businesses. This is okay, but that doesn't mean you have to listen to them.

These people seem to actually want to crush your dreams. They may be a friend who doesn't want to lose you to something else, they may not fully appreciate your dreams, or they may simply be like crabs in a bucket, just pulling anyone down who tries to get out. Remember that most people are obsessed with job security and are not entrepreneurial; consider this before taking their opinion seriously.

We don't need pessimists judging our business ideas right out of the gate. Knowing when to ignore these people is important. These days, even if I think something is a bad idea, I'm more likely to say, "Hmm, that might work, but I would test it with some potential customers first." And how would I or anyone know until it was tested?

Top Reasons for Failure

Also, let's remind ourselves at this point of why most startups fail, not to discourage you, but so you can keep your eye on these issues and recognize them when you see them. As I mentioned previously, simply being aware of these problems and not making big startup mistakes can increase your chances of success.

Now, the Founder Superpowers in Part One we've gone over will help prevent many problems, but these are the big reasons that many entrepreneurs identify *after* their startup has failed. Generally, the top reasons for failure are in a few broad categories that are many times closely related:

Reason #1: Product Market Fit

This reason is so obvious now that many startup gurus just shorten it to PMF. If there's not a market for your product or service, then you're going to have a hard time. This is why testing ideas before plunging in is so valuable; try your best to determine PMF before you even launch. This also includes products with low margins (people not willing to pay enough for them).

Note that I will also include "running out of cash" in this category because if people don't want your product, then they're not going to give you cash for it. Also, timing is related to this as well. The Startups Made Simple Business Plan will force you to think through PMF, test your idea, and hopefully avoid this landmine.

Reason #2: People Problems

This is a broad category that includes everything from the wrong co-founder(s) to the wrong first hires. The basic lesson is this: Do you want to work with these people day in and out through possibly very challenging times?

Picking the wrong co-founder(s) will sink your company so fast that I rarely recommend any team split ownership in the company equally; this helps ensure the company is not deadlocked into a dispute that could end it. If each owner has 50%, for example, and disagree, then the result can be catastrophic. Even a 49/51 split is better.

You should have this discussion with any potential co-founder before you start the company, and get something in writing about who will own what. In addition, I recommend listing the areas of responsibility and the hours or deliverables required by each founder. Some founders just take off after a while and contribute nothing, while the others are working 80-hour weeks, which will really hurt some feelings. In the resources, I've listed some good articles on splitting ownership equity and an overview of stock options.

Pick your co-founder based on whether you like them, can see yourself working with them forever, and are honest enough to tell each other the truth and resolve issues in a healthy manner. Many friends start companies and won't tell each other the honest truth, which causes problems.

Your first hires are also important, but not as critical as the founder issue. We'll go over hiring and management best practices in Step 5, but I will remind you that the first hires are important and may set the culture for the company going forward. Don't ignore that and simply hire the first person who walks in the door.

Finally, the complexity of employment law is very risky for startups, so I always encourage startups to consider outsourcing all non-core functions of the business. Only hire for the critical functions. It's amazing what remote contractors can accomplish for your company (basically anything that can be done via computer or phone).

Reason #3: Product/Service Problems

This is also a broad category, but sometimes an entrepreneur will have a great idea yet their implementation will be poor and kill the company. Sometimes, I see entrepreneurs with great ideas and clear plans, but the execution is not well done, and the product or service doesn't live up to the expectations.

This reason is related to people problems as well as sometimes hiring bad people or having the wrong co-founder(s) and will be the source behind the product/service problems. Imagine bad hires giving poor service or a co-founder's bad management skills causing implementation problems.

Reason #4: Poor Marketing/Sales

I get disagreement on this issue from some because they think that a great product or service sells itself, and sometimes that is true. But as a general rule, a lot of founders are really a product or service expert but have not learned to properly promote and sell, which is a hugely valuable skill.

Some people think it's scammy or uncool to toot your own horn, but I believe that's just silly. I used to think that way myself but now know that it mostly doesn't matter how great your product or service is if nobody knows about it. We all know the great restaurant or shop that shocked us by suddenly going out of business; I can usually assume they didn't focus enough on sales and marketing. In Step 4, we'll go deeply into this to hopefully prevent this problem.

Lessons for Avoiding Failure

What easy lesson is there to be learned? You want to:

1. Test, then build and obsess about a great product or service that people want and will pay enough money for to support a real business

2. Partner with and hire great people from the start who you wouldn't mind working with forever

3. Learn the Founder Superpowers and also add sales and marketing skills to your skillset

The Name and Initial Branding

Now, let's move on to the exciting things like picking a name for this idea. Few topics can get as argumentative as the importance or unimportance of naming and branding at this point in a business idea.

Many will disagree with me, but I think the name and initial branding of the company is pretty important but not worth obsessing over for more than a few days. I've seen entrepreneurs waste weeks or longer on this (it's a great excuse for procrastinating), so don't make that mistake, but definitely put some solid thinking into it.

Why? For example, I'm now on my third company name and a few hours of strategic thinking would have prevented the hundreds of wasted hours in rebranding, legal filings, domain/email name change, etc. each time. I started out with Bold New Enterprise as a company that helped start new companies. I soon found out that customers were saying Enterprises and didn't fully understand the name, so I changed it to MyNewCompany.com.

This was the second mistake. We eventually did more than just form new companies, so it never really described that we've become this full-service business entity formation and management company. We had to change it again to MyCompanyWorks which I love, and I believe will survive the growth of the company to encompass many possible futures and products or services.

Here's another example: Say you wanted to start a company that did financial planning for individuals and businesses. Of the two names/brands below, which would you immediately trust more:

Fast Eddie's Financial Services, Inc.
Integrity Financial Services, Inc.

This is obviously an unfair comparison, but I hope you get my point: The name, font, and coloring can convey more than you may realize. Be mindful of perception. Have I ever done business with a company only because of a logo or name? No. Have I looked through a bunch of companies to do business with and rejected one because of an unprofessional name or homemade logo? Absolutely. Or worse, my brain has rejected a company because of a perception I can't even articulate, a feeling of something being off.

This may just be me, but don't discount my opinion on this. You don't need an expensive logo or branding package; just make sure the name makes sense, meets the basics, and the logo is decent and looks good across where you'll use it and in monochrome (and looks good square if you intend to use it online as an avatar on social media).

The counter-argument is that it's silly to waste time on the name, and you'll discover that even a silly name like Google will eventually reveal itself as cool and could become a worldwide brand. Again, I respect this argument. I'm simply making the point that you should spend a few hours thinking about it but not obsess over it.

With that cautionary tale out of the way, here are the best practices I know of for picking a company (or product) name:

1. **Don't obsess on the name**. As discussed, spend some time on the name and maybe even colors, but if it's not coming to you quickly, don't obsess over it, and just pick a name that's good enough. If you can't think of any name, just give your idea a code name like Project Alpha so you can clear your mental bandwidth to focus on your plan and testing. Giving it *some* name is important because it will give your idea more life, and it becomes more real that way. An exception to this rule might be a consumer product or restaurant where having a cool name is imperative; then it's worth spending the time.

2. **Conveys what the business does.** One of the big arguments is should you name it something made up like

Flooshie or just name it what the company will do? My opinion is that it's very hard (and usually expensive) to build a brand name from nothing, so you'll likely be better off as "Integrity Financial Services" vs "IntegraServ" if only for the simple fact that a person is more likely to understand what your company does without explanation. Also, it's easier to own the word in your target market's head if it's actually relevant to the market.

3. **Pronounceable and clear.** Make sure it's pronounceable. Actually say it out loud like you're answering the phone for your company. Amazon.com, Inc. found out their initial name "Cadabra" sounded like "cadaver." "Symmetry" sounds like cemetery, etc. Also, some names are not clear about pronunciation, so make sure that the average person can read it and pronounce it correctly.

4. **Can survive growth.** Like my personal example above, many people make the mistake of choosing to focus on one aspect of the product or service but don't realize they may grow to sell related or other products or services eventually. So "ABC Home Services, Inc." would be superior to "ABC Vacuum Repair Services, Inc." because the latter name would be limiting or irrelevant. Note that you can also always file a fictitious name or "Doing Business As" (discussed in the next chapter) to quickly resolve this problem, so again, it's not worth obsessing over but something to think about.

5. **Simple font and color.** Again, we're not going crazy here, but open up your word processor and play around with the colors and fonts on your new name to get a feel for what would work best. If inclined, search for "business colors" online to see the psychology of certain colors (business = blue, orange = new, etc.) or types of business personas (friendly, professional, goofy, etc.) or similar brands you like and respect.

6. **Test the name.** Once you've settled on a name (or several), test them just like you will the business idea itself. Send it to potential customers to get critical feedback. Many times, ideas that seem awesome to us may not make sense to others.

7. **Available and simple domain name.** This isn't so hard anymore with the explosion of available Top Level Domains (TLDs) other than .com (.co, .biz, etc.), but if you're hard set on a .com, you'll want to do a quick search online to verify the domain name is available. Also, I've seen people do incredibly long or hard-to-spell domain names that are not user-friendly (hard for people to remember or tell via phone); either abbreviate or focus on a different TLD.

8. **Quick trademark search.** You can go to USPTO.gov and do a quick search on your name. This is to avoid a legal landmine right from the beginning. At this point, we're just looking for obvious conflicts and can do a much more thorough search later (which can be somewhat complex).

9. **Quick state name search.** Google can help you find the Secretary of State business name database in each state. Do a quick search to find any obvious conflicts.

10. **Consistency.** After the company or product is launched, one simple thing to do that demonstrates competence (in my opinion) is being consistent with your colors, fonts, and even the "voice" in which you write. This means websites, email signatures, letterheads, etc. should be consistent across your company.

The Startups Made Simple Business Plan

"A good plan violently executed now is better than a perfect plan next week." —General George S. Patton

All right, you have a business idea, you're aware of the landmines discussed above, and it's now time to begin testing. This is where the Startups Made Simple Business Plan comes into play. We're going to force you to think through the idea. Your number-one goal is to learn from potential customers so you can validate this business idea.

Long-term business planning is not required for the vast majority of business ideas, especially small businesses. Frankly, your plan is just a guess, and the best way you can guess is to get real feedback from real potential customers. You may find out that many of these ideas may not work as planned, and if so, keep iterating or trying new ideas.

Trying out many bad ideas is better than never even attempting anything. You want to start tinkering with your ideas and not put so much value into the idea, just the testing and execution. As discussed, many famous entrepreneurs dismissed dozens or even hundreds of ideas.

Vision and Elevator Pitch

So your Startups Made Simple Business Plan starts with writing a quick paragraph on what your product or service clearly does. Feel free to write out a lot more to begin with, but then try to refine it to a few sentences or even one sentence if possible.

You've probably heard of the famous elevator pitch, and that's what you want: a quick simple way to explain and sell your idea to anyone who will listen. If the idea is too complicated to explain quickly, that might be a warning sign of unnecessary complexity or that you need to take another pass at simplifying your idea.

Target Market

Next, let's define who this product or service is built for. Who is the exact customer for this, and where would you find them? The standard who, what, where, and why questions apply here. You might know this by being an expert in the product already, or you might need to do lots of research.

Mostly, you want to define the ideal customer for this product, so we can somehow get this idea in their face and get their opinion on it. This doesn't have to be perfect now, but try to get as detailed as possible so you can really drill down to someone who will actually use your product or service.

Similar to the RAS as discussed in Step 1, we want to identify our target market and begin putting our brain to work learning how to find and identify these people. We'll want to know their dreams, frustrations, how they work, and more. See Step 4 for more details on this.

Brainstorm Tests to Run

This will be heavily dependent on which type of business you want to start, but there are many ways to test an idea:

1. **Share It.** Try to share it with potential customers or even vendors, suppliers, etc. who might supply you or help build your product. As we discussed in Step 1, the risk of somebody stealing the idea is overblown, but practice caution if you suspect anyone might steal the concept. Try to talk to someone in the industry and be aware of the ups and downs, but don't let them poison you; they may be jaded. You'd be amazed at how many people will respond to a cold email offering to take them to lunch to get their insight on an idea.

2. **Surveys**. Create a simple survey and send it to potential customers. Be sure to ask if they would pay for this and how much they would pay.

3. **Mockup**. You can make a drawing or mockup of the product, website, machine or whatever you're trying to build. Let people get a nice visual of what you're trying to build, and they'll be more likely to tell you the truth if they'd pay for it. For example, if you have an idea for a TV/radio show, take out your phone, record a show, upload it to YouTube and monitor the reaction.

4. **Press Release**. Made famous by Jeff Bezos, he'll sometimes have a team write up a press release before the product is built. This makes you think about not only how the end product will look and feel but gives you a head start on how you would market it.

5. **Website**. Modern website building software is "point and click," and a good website can be mocked up in hours. Consider building out a basic website for this product and service as if it were real and live now, then send that around to your target market for feedback or a survey.

6. **Advertise**. You can create a survey or website online (as mentioned above) and then buy some test ads on Google, Facebook, or other places and actually target potential customers by location, interest, and keywords they're searching for.

7. **Prototype or Minimum Viable Product (MVP)**. Build a minimum working version of the product so people can actually use it. This is probably the best way to get real feedback as you will be able so survey real users of your product. Tip: Ask them how disappointed they would be if your product didn't exist. If they say "very disappointed" or similar, that's a great sign that your product is valuable. Jim Koch of Sam Adams brewery made batches of beer at his house and went to local bars giving samples to get his business launched.

Test, Analyze, and Repeat

"Don't worry, be crappy. Revolutionary means you ship and then test. Lots of things made the first Mac in 1984 a piece of crap – but it was a revolutionary piece of crap."
—Guy Kawasaki

Now we just need to run our test or tests and start to get feedback. It's important for you to avoid perfectionism while testing. Your mockup might look crappy, and that's okay for now. It's perfectly fine to have cheesy, terrible designs at this point because we're just looking for feedback.

As mentioned in Step 1, there are several indicators of a winning idea but a really good one is having a potential customer basically tell you to "shut up and take my money!" When you have 5–10 people saying this, that's probably a pretty good sign. This isn't foolproof, of course, because sometimes people won't tell you the truth (especially friends and family), so the important thing is to really get someone to commit to saying they'd actually pay for this right now if it existed.

You might start out with a simple survey that you can make online, send it around, see the feedback, and then move on to a mockup, website, or even an MVP to further clarify and get feedback. When I first launched my company, I had a friend build me a very simple online order form, and I actually placed some Internet ads to see if I could get some orders. I did and this immediately let me know I'd hit on a viable idea. The first website to sell cars, CarsDirect, actually sold some cars this way, simply to prove that people would buy cars online before driving them.

The point is to closely analyze the feedback, move forward, tweak, retest, or decide that this idea simply has no traction, and if not, go back to the drawing board. Don't get discouraged if this happens. This is just part of the regular entrepreneurial process of coming up with ideas and tossing out the vast majority that will not work. We're simply making this process faster and much less risky by testing first. Having your ideas shot down sucks, but wasting years on a bad idea is much worse, trust me. Remember Einstein and Edison who had hundreds of dismissed ideas.

Back of the Napkin Math

You want to at the least take an educated guess on how much money you could make with your idea, so do some quick math to make sure your business will not only pay the bills, but help you thrive and build wealth. Doing this can prevent some big mistakes down the road; many people were simply never aware of the basic financials before starting.

This is not as hard as it sounds, you want to start out by estimating your current monthly expenses to live at your current lifestyle. (Or perhaps you could skimp in the startup phase and dial things down a bit, the so-called "ramen money" that lets you get by.) Let's say you need $4,000/month in expenses. Next, take whatever you're selling (product, service, consulting, etc.) and estimate what the profit would be per unit, hour or whatever.

For example, if I'm starting a consulting or service business and I'll charge $50/hour, I know that I need at least 80 billable hours a month (plus any expenses I incur) to meet my current lifestyle. If I'm selling a widget for $50, I know I need to sell 80 per month (plus the wholesale or manufacturing cost, which can be considerable and drastically change the math, so don't ignore it). If I'm selling a recurring service for $50/month, I need 80 subscribers per month. You get my point here. Do so some basic math, and you'll discover just how feasible the financials are on your idea.

Ready to Launch?

If your idea has passed the test phase to your satisfaction, it's time to start your company. The next chapter, Step 3, will give you the step-by-step instructions for getting this business started, but there are a few planning issues you should consider now before pulling the trigger on your new venture:

1. **Funding**. If you believe you have enough money to fund your new company, then this is not a concern. However, if you will need to get funding from either a bank, investors, or even a venture capital firm then you'll possibly need to consider a formal professional business plan and begin research on the proper way to pitch investors. I cover the basics in the next chapter, but there's a lot of information about this online and the market for money is constantly changing with crowdfunding and other money raising tools.

2. **Long-Term Items**. Some business plans require things that may take a long time. For example, building a business location, building out a restaurant, manufacturing a product, getting various complex government approvals, and similar items. Make sure you include these in your plan so you can begin at least researching the requirements.

3. **Overcome Resistance**. This is where fear sometimes creeps in, and a lot of entrepreneurs fall off the wagon. Review the Superpowers in Part 1, and remember that not only is none of this permanent, it's just an experiment that could fail, but you'll certainly learn lessons and potentially hit it big. It's just business, and they can't eat you.

4. **Backup Plan**. It's always wise to think a bit about the worst case scenario if things go wrong with this business. It sounds counterintuitive, but this tends to actually relax you and help you think of possible alternative paths if this exact idea doesn't work out as planned. For example, if my product X doesn't sell, then I could pivot to Y or do consulting in the industry or get my old job back at Z. Or, if my retail location doesn't make it, I'm going to insist on an escape or sub-lease clause in my lease so I'm not stuck for several years of payments, etc. List out the possible bad items and come up with ways to mitigate them as much as possible.

MATT KNEE

So are we ready to launch?
Onward!

Visit http://www.startupsmadesimple.com for Chapter 6 Resources and to download the Startups Made Simple Business Plan.

7
STEP THREE: START IT

"An idea that is developed and put into action is more important than an idea that exists only as an idea."
—Buddha

All right, we're getting close now. You've come up with your idea, you're reasonably confident it will succeed, and you've at least done some basic testing and "back of the napkin" math. You're ready to go! In this step, you'll go through a checklist of items that may *seem* boring but are actually very exciting as the imaginary becomes real.

Formal Business Plan or Not

In Step 2, we went over a Startups Made Simple Business Plan, and that is going to be just fine for probably over 90% of startups.

However, if there are complexities in your business or you intend to get funding from banks, angel investors, or venture capitalists, they're likely going to require a more comprehensive business plan (of which there are dozens of free examples online) or at least a pitch deck presentation covering things like:

- Executive Summary
- Description of the Problem
- Your Solution
- Market Size
- The Business Model (how you'll make money)
- Competitors
- Your Competitive Advantage
- Founder Biographies
- Marketing Plan
- Fundraising
- Detailed Use of Funds

As I mentioned in Step 2, there are so many sources of funding these days and the market is moving so fast that if I covered all the ways to raise funds now, it would be outdated by the time this book was published. Also, less than 1% of companies ever get venture capital, so I don't focus on VC in this book. That said, here's a list of potential sources of funding and the chapter resources will also list specific sources:

- Bootstrapping (Personal funds, being resourceful and frugal, DIY)
- Credit Cards
- Friends and Family

- Home Equity Loans
- Personal Notes or Loans from a Bank
- Cashing in Pensions, IRA's, 401ks, etc.
- Angel Investors
- Federal, State, or Local Grants
- Startup Incubators (private or public)
- Crowdfunding (Kickstarter, GoFundMe)
- Small Business Administration (SBA) Loans

Decide and Clarify Ownership Issues Before Starting

In the Founder Superpowers section of this book on making good decisions, as well as Step 2 in Top Reasons for Failure, I mentioned that nothing will sink a company faster than ownership issues if you have more than one founder. Fights, disagreements, misunderstood expectations, and more can paralyze or destroy your company, so let's list out the issues that you should address in writing before you even form the company.

A good rule of thumb is that if you don't want to work with these people forever, then don't work with them at all. Sure, these may be uncomfortable to bring up now, but this could save a lot of grief later.

- Founders should agree on the ownership percentage before they even create the company.

- Founders should try to avoid 50/50 or other equal splits of ownership that may paralyze a company in case of disagreement. Even 51/49 is better than 50/50 as it lets one owner have veto power. Flip a coin if necessary.

- Founders should agree to how much work is minimally required to earn their percentage of ownership. You don't want some founders working 10 hours a week while others are working 50. You don't want one founder around for only a few months and still owning half the company 5 years later.

- You can make the agreement stipulate that an owner needs to sell back their ownership if they don't abide by the agreement.

- Founders should agree on what specific responsibilities and decisions should be made by each, preferably with deadlines. For example, one founder develops the product while the other manages employees and handles marketing.

You can make your own document, have signed copies given to all founders, and that would be good, but this is one place an attorney could help greatly. For corporations, a Shareholders Agreement is typically what this called but basically it's an agreement among owners. It can be simple or very complex covering issues like intellectual property, valuation, selling back shares, what happens when a founder dies, etc.

Decide on Stock Options or Equity Grants

Another thing I want you to consider before we go to file the official company paperwork is if you will ever want to grant stock options or ownership in your company. If so, then you should be aware of how much expense and complexity this will add to your company. There are services that assist with this now, and it's much easier to manage than in the past, but adding a proper stock option program to your company definitely requires an attorney and is difficult to administer.

Stock option programs require fairly complex valuations, things like an 83(b) election with the IRS, vesting schedules, and more. It's not something I'd recommend to your average self-funded startup, but if you need this, then you definitely want to have an attorney assist with the setup (and perhaps management) of the program.

What's the alternative to complex schemes like that? First, you can give ownership away as a gift without paying the Federal Gift Tax (currently up to $15,000 year per person). For example, you could give 1% away per year to a valued employee. Also, so-called "phantom stock" plans are becoming more popular. Phantom stock plans are a simple agreement that if the company has a liquidity event (company is sold, acquired, etc.) or even a certain profit, that person X will receive Y percent of the total value; otherwise, they recieve and are entitled to nothing. Now both of these options will also require an attorney to setup but they're much simpler than a proper stock option program and don't require constant management.

Select a Name and Legal Structure

Now that we're clear on potential ownership issues and the complexity of various stock and ownership schemes, it's time to file the paperwork to create our business. As mentioned in Step 2, don't obsess about the business name, just pick one, and let's file the paperwork. Read Step 2 to see more best practices in picking your business name and doing a preliminary name and trademark search. The name can always be changed and so can the legal structure, but let's go over some of the basics so you can make the choice.

For the vast majority of entrepreneurs, you'll choose one of the following three legal structures or business entities. Note that this information is relevant for forming a business entity in the United States (whether you're a U.S. citizen or not).

Option 1: DBA/FBN

A DBA or FBN (also known as a sole proprietorship, Doing Business As, or a Fictitious Business Name; these names vary by state) is a business that is not separate from its owner, merely a different name that the business owner operates under. The owner is personally liable for the company and its debt; all income is added on the owner(s) personal tax returns (pass-through taxation). If there is more than one owner, then the business is classified as a General Partnership.

Taxation: Simple taxation. You add your income (or losses) to your personal 1040 tax return in a separate schedule (if more than one partner then each person gets their own schedule). Even TurboTax can handle the vast majority of DBA taxes.

Pros: Easy to set up, easy to maintain.

Cons: Owners are personally liable for the company and its debt (could lose their house, cars, personal assets, etc.) in a lawsuit. Usually not recognized at the state level, only in your city/county. No corporate "prestige" of having the "Inc." or "LLC" attached to your name. LLC's have primarily replaced DBAs as the entity of choice for even the smallest businesses.

NOTE: If you form a corporation or LLC, you can also file a DBA for your company, which means your corporation or LLC can do business under different names as well. This is ideal if you want to have one company that does multiple lines of business. For example, if you are ABC Services, LLC you can file a DBA as "Dave's T-Shirts" and another DBA as "Dave's Landscaping".

Option 2: Corporation ("S Corporation" or "C Corporation")

A corporation is a separate legal entity that can shield the owners from personal liability and company debt. As a separate entity, it can buy real estate, enter into contracts, and sue and be sued completely separately from its owners. Also, money can be raised easier via the sale of stock; its ownership can be transferred via the transfer of stock; the duration of the corporation is perpetual (the business can continue regardless of ownership); and the tax advantages can be considerable (i.e. you are able to deduct many business expenses, healthcare programs, etc. that other legal entities are not). Income is reported completely separate via a tax return for the corporation.

A corporation is set up in this structure:

- Shareholders own the stock of the corporation
- Shareholders elect directors (known as the Board of Directors)
- Directors appoint officers (president, secretary, treasurer, etc.)
- Officers run the company (day-to-day operations)

In many cases (especially during the startup phase), you will be the 100% owner of the stock; therefore, you elect the directors (usually yourself) and then appoint yourself as an officer (or all the officers: CEO, treasurer, secretary).

The rules for operating your corporation are set in what are called corporate bylaws. This document sets the rules for the company and can be modified as the business grows and changes.

Operating a corporation involves, at the minimum, holding a yearly directors and shareholders meeting (the location is determined by you and the expenses are deductible), keeping written minutes of major company decisions, and maintaining general corporate compliance as dictated by the corporate bylaws.

A C-corporation is what all corporations are by default, you are automatically a C-corporation unless you specifically elect to be an S-corporation. You can choose to be an S-corporation by filing a form with the IRS (and some states require a separate form). "S" means "Small" corporation, which is restricted to U.S. citizens and a limited number of shareholders, currently under 100. S-corporations also may not own or be owned by other business entities (important to consider if you want to own "subsidiary" companies through one business entity).

Taxation: The most complex of the three options. Both an S-corporation and a C-corporation require a fairly complex separate tax return (separate from your personal 1040 return). Some simple companies can get away with using a service like TurboTax but most usually require the assistance of an accountant or CPA. C-corporations are taxed twice: You pay taxes on the profits, then you pay taxes again when the profits are given to each shareholder. The majority of small corporations are S-corporations because it means you do not pay a separate corporate tax on your profits, which is currently at 21%.

Pros: The oldest, most successful, and most prestigious type of business entity; provides personal liability protection; conveys permanence, can reduce taxes (lower tax rate on retained profits, items like healthcare, travel and entertainment are deductible).

Cons: More expensive to set up than a DBA; more paperwork and formality required than an LLC (holding shareholder/board meetings, keeping minutes and resolutions).

Option 3: Limited Liability Company (LLC)

A limited liability company can be best described as a hybrid between a corporation and a partnership. It provides easy management and pass-through taxation (profits and losses are added to the owner(s) personal tax returns) like a sole proprietorship/partnership, with similar liability protection of a corporation. It's a relatively new form of business created in 1977 in Wyoming and now recognized in all fifty states and D.C.

Like a corporation, it is a separate legal entity; unlike a corporation, there is no stock, and there are fewer formalities. The owners of an LLC are called "members" instead of "shareholders."

In essence, it's like a corporation with less complicated taxation and stock formalities.

The heart of a limited liability company is known as the Operating Agreement. This document sets the rules for operating the company and can be modified as the business grows and changes.

Operating an LLC is less formal than a corporation, usually only requiring an annual members meeting and members' agreeing to changes of the operating agreement and other major company decisions.

Taxation: Simple or complex. The beauty of the LLC is that by default it's taxed just like a DBA/FBN: You just add your income or losses to your personal 1040 tax return, very simple. You can also elect to have it taxed like an S-corporation or C-corporation if you want a more advanced tax setup but this is pretty rare for small businesses.

Pros: Provides the liability protection of a corporation without the corporate formalities (board meetings, shareholder meetings, minutes, etc.) and extra levels of management (shareholders, directors, officers). Taxed the same as a sole proprietorship (one-member LLC) or partnership (two or more members) by default.

Cons: Usually more expensive to form than a DBA, requires more paperwork and formal behavior.

Options for Non-US Citizens

About 20% of our clients at MyCompanyWorks, Inc. are now international, so we specialize in their unique circumstances. There are some important details to be aware of if you're not a U.S. Citizen.

1. You must file either an LLC or a C-corporation. S-corporations are restricted to U.S. citizens only.

2. Typically you have to live in the county to file a DBA/FBN. So if you just need a U.S. entity you'll likely need a C-corporation or LLC.

3. The only requirement to form an LLC or C-corporation for a non-U.S. Citizen is to hire a registered agent to be your official address (my company provides this in all U.S. states, see the Chapter Resources for more).

4. Getting a Federal Employer Identification Number (FEIN) is required of all companies and is more complicated if you don't have any owner with a Social Security Number. It delays the process by a few weeks but can be done as long as you are aware you'll need to obtain an International Tax Identification Number (ITIN) by the next year when taxes are due.

5. Getting a bank account for non-U.S. Citizens has become incredibly difficult since 9/11 and various "know your customer" laws have been implemented. Many times, a quick visit to the U.S. or the local branch of a U.S. bank is required to open the account.

Picking a State for Your Corporation or LLC

One of the unique features of incorporating or forming an LLC is that you do not necessarily have to form the company in the state where you do business. When deciding on which state to incorporate in, there are basically two choices:

Your Home State

For the vast majority of small businesses, incorporating or forming an LLC in your home state is usually the easiest and least expensive option. This is because virtually every state has laws that require you to re-register a Delaware or Nevada company in the state where it is actually doing business.

For example, if you form a Nevada corporation but your physical business is located in Colorado, the state of Colorado will want you to re-register as what's called a "foreign corporation" (a company that was not originally incorporated in Colorado). This is especially true if you intend to get a bank account and business license or rent office space in your home state.

In most cases, registering as a foreign corporation or LLC will subject you to all the same taxes and fees as an in-state company, so you will probably have not avoided any taxes or fees, plus there is the added expense of registering as a foreign corporation in your home state and any annual fees in both states.

This is not to say there are not valid reasons for choosing another state, I just want you to be aware of the additional steps required when choosing a state outside of your home state. Further discussion with your attorney or other advisor is recommended.

Delaware, Nevada or Wyoming

Delaware

Delaware is where most large corporations (Fortune 500, Nasdaq, etc.) are incorporated. The reason for this is that Delaware's body of law is more business-oriented, and they have a large and advanced business court system (called the Chancery court) to handle complex legal litigation. It is the state of choice for both large corporations, foreign corporations, and many fast-growing or high-potential companies. For example, venture capitalists typically require a Delaware corporation before they'll invest in your company.

Nevada

Nevada has recently exploded in popularity for both large and small businesses. This is due to Nevada's very pro-business climate, low-tax mentality, and the lack of an information-sharing agreement with the IRS (all other states share company information with the IRS).

Pros:
- No corporate income tax
- No franchise tax
- No state personal income tax
- Stockholders are not a matter of public record (though officers, directors and members of LLCs are)
- Nevada corporations and LLCs are legendary for being difficult to pierce the "corporate veil." This means that it is extremely difficult for attorneys to go after the company owners, shareholders, officers, or directors personal assets in a lawsuit; it's only happened a handful of times in recent history.
- In states like California, the corporate veil is regularly pierced in a large percentage of lawsuits, so you could lose your house, cars, etc. in a lawsuit. In many cases, simply having a Nevada corporation or LLC may be enough to ward off a lawsuit or predatory lawyers.
- Nevada has a very pro-business climate with no information sharing agreement with the IRS.
- Officers, directors and members need not be U.S. citizens or residents of Nevada.
- Minimal annual requirements: all you need to do on an annual basis is maintain a Nevada registered agent and file your annual list/state business license.

Cons:
- Nevada has recently raised their filing fees, which are now higher than Delaware and significantly more than Wyoming.
- You may have to re-register your Nevada company in the state where you operate (if you're not based in Nevada or have not established "nexus").
- There are legitimate ways to obtain nexus for your company in Nevada as your primary source of operations, but

we highly recommend further discussion with an attorney in this matter.

Wyoming
Wyoming has also recently exploded in popularity for its very business-friendly climate and has been called the Switzerland of the Rocky Mountains by *The Economist* magazine. It features some benefits compared to a Nevada entity including:

- Wyoming was actually the first state to create the LLC in 1977.
- All the benefits of Nevada listed above but much lower filing fees
- Lower annual fees
- Minimal annual requirements: All you need to do on an annual basis is maintain a Wyoming registered agent and file your annual report.
- Does not require listing the members of an LLC or the shareholders of a corporation.
- Does not require a state business license (Nevada does, even if you operate out of state).

Common Reasons for Choosing Delaware, Wyoming, or Nevada

- **Prestige**: A Delaware entity is the chosen business entity of the largest, most successful and fastest-growing companies in the world.
- **Protection**: Predatory consumers or lawyers who attempt to threaten companies may be more hesitant to deal with a Nevada, Wyoming, or Delaware company knowing that the body of law protecting the company may be more business friendly and protect the owners/shareholders

more effectively. Also, the identity of the company owners may be more difficult to ascertain.

- **Convenience**: In some cases, a business may find itself moving from state to state or having partners all over the country. In this case, some businesses find it easier to simply use a Nevada, Wyoming, or Delaware entity as a sort of headquarters that maintains the company while it moves or expands to other states. This can be easier than continuously creating and dissolving in-state companies (and changing tax ID numbers, registered agent addresses, losing company credit profiles, etc.)

- **High-growth or high-risk company**: If your company is fast-growing or engaged in a risky industry (such as fireworks or children's toys), then Nevada, Wyoming, or Delaware may provide the liability protection you need. Also, if your company is fast-growing, choosing Delaware now may prevent you from needing to inevitably re-incorporate there in the future when your company needs to go public or receive venture funding, etc.

- **Holding property or independent contractor**: A client who simply needs an entity and a bank account to purchase or hold property, accept payments as a contractor, or receive investment money will form a Delaware, Nevada, or Wyoming company for this purpose since they are really not operating a business in their home state.

- **Managing side projects**: Many people like to use a business entity to keep side projects organized under one entity.

The Lowdown on Picking a Business Entity and State

Much like obsessing over the business name, it's not worth obsessing much over the business entity or state which can always be changed later (things are easier if you don't have to change, but it's not that hard). Facebook famously started out as a Florida LLC but is now a Delaware C-corporation (like most big U.S. companies).

Here are some basic guidelines to make your decision easier:

1. If you intend to get venture capital, then you will almost certainly be required to be formed as a Delaware C-corporation.

2. If you don't intend to move states, all founders are in the same state, you don't intend to get venture capital and the business is not risky, then the state where you live is probably the obvious choice.

3. Non-U.S. citizens need to choose an LLC or C-corporation. Picking the state would be a matter of convenience if you don't live in the U.S., don't intend to get venture capital (which would likely require a Delaware C corporation), or the business is not risky.

4. A lot of people try to get creative in their business setup with complex ownership and business entity schemes (e.g. an LLC holding company owns several corporations that each own various parts of the company). I can say that I've literally never seen this scenario work out as expected nor worth the additional expense and complexity for a small startup.

5. Each situation is different. Speak to an attorney if you have any hesitation. Even one hour of advice can clear up any questions or concerns about these fairly complex scenarios.

6. Remember that business names, entities, and even states can be changed. None of this is written in stone. Focus more on your actual business than the business name or structure.

How to File Your Business Entity

Most people go to an attorney, an online service like my company or do the paperwork themselves. DBA/FBNs can typically be filed with your county clerk and they usually have the forms available online or in-person. Corporations and LLCs are typically filed with the Secretary of State and also have the forms available online or in-person.

Typically the forms are pretty easy to complete after you search the name for availability, which is somewhat of an art itself. You'll pay a filing fee to submit the form then wait anywhere from a day to several weeks depending on the county or state.

The form will either be accepted or rejected. If it's accepted, you're basically in business and it's time to continue doing the other checklist items below. Some states have requirements that your new business be published in a newspaper and will provide those instructions with your filing.

Obtain Your Federal Employer Identification Number (FEIN)

If you are setup as a corporation, LLC, or partnership (or a sole proprietorship with employees), apply for a Federal Employer Identification Number (FEIN) from the IRS by filing Form SS-4 or filing it out online. A FEIN will be necessary to open a bank account or process payroll. Think of your FEIN as the Social Security Number for your company.

Open the Company Bank Account

It's important to separate your personal and business expenses (for proper accounting and legal compliance), so select a bank and open the company bank account. Most people just choose the same bank where they have a personal account. If you're going to get a loan or otherwise have specific needs from a bank, do your research and select the right one for your business. Typically, to open the account, you will need your filed company paperwork, your FEIN paperwork, and perhaps an application or written document authorizing the various owners, officers, etc. to make transactions.

Tip: Contact the bank prior to opening the account to see what their specific requirements are to open a business checking account. Some banks' requirements are fairly simple whereas some banks' requirements are extremely complex.

Organize and Capitalize the Company

Now that you have a company bank account, it's time to put money into the company so you can capitalize the company and start paying for business expenses through a proper business bank account. Note that you can reimburse any expenses incurred by the founders before the account was established. How much money you need to put in the company depends on how much you are capable of, (some states have a $1,000 minimum), but the general rule of thumb is to put enough cash in the company to get you operational and cover your startup expenses for a while. You can always inject additional cash later.

If you are setup as a DBA/FBN and are a sole owner, this process is very simple; simply move money into your business account and that's your startup capital. If you are a DBA/FBN with more than one founder, the same basic process applies but you'll want to get in writing who has contributed what and who owns what percentage of the company i. Typically, this is called a Partnership Agreement and can be very simple, even one page. Search online; there are many examples.

If you are setup as a corporation, you will exchange money (and sometimes services or past expenses used in the formation of the company) for stock. Put money in your company bank account, and the company will issue stock to you as proof of your ownership in the company. You will keep track of stock ownership using what's called a Stock Ledger (basically a spreadsheet). Even if you're a one-person company, this process still applies. It's how you'll prove ownership of your company and even transfer or sell it later.

Corporations should hold what's called an Organizational Meeting where they will issue this stock and also complete the setup of the company including electing directors and officers, adopting the corporate bylaws, and other post-formation tasks. Whomever handled the filing of your corporation will typically provide you with forms or templates for all of the above and some guidance on completing these important steps. Note that these steps are important. Don't just file your paperwork to form the company and then not properly organize the company afterward; this could have severe consequences later. Finally, if there are multiple shareholders, consider having them all sign a Shareholders Agreement as mentioned earlier in this chapter.

LLCs should hold an Organizational Meeting as well. The main difference is that LLCs are typically set up to exchange ownership percentage instead of stock. This means that the process is very similar to a DBA/FBN: Put money in the bank and track who owns what. LLC's typically have what's called an Operating Agreement that also details ownership percentage and has various rules on transferring ownership, meetings, how to handle disputes, etc., which is important especially if there are multiple owners. Some LLCs can be set up to use units of ownership, which are similar to stock but are somewhat complex and beyond the scope of this book. (Talk to your advisor if you want this option.) You will keep track of LLC ownership using what's called a Member Ledger (again, basically a spreadsheet).

All of the documents mentioned above should be organized centrally in a company binder. Corporations and LLCs can get what's called a Minute Book that has the forms and Ledgers mentioned above as well as proper Stock or Member Certificates and a Seal to stamp official company documents.

Shameless Self Promotion

If you know the type of company you want and where you want to file it you can spend hours doing the previous tasks I've mentioned above or you can go to my company's website at www.mycompanyworks.com and spend about ten minutes on an order form and let us handle it like we've done for over 50,000 clients since 2001. We form companies in all 50 states and D.C. We search the name with the state, file your paperwork (correctly!), provide a registered agent (if necessary), provide the post-formation organizational documents ready for signature, provide a Minute Book and even guidance on the bank account, business licenses and an interactive checklist called the Startup Wizard to help you do the remaining setup tasks. The only thing we can't offer is financial, legal or tax advice so if you need any of that, ask an advisor first.

Arrange Office, Warehouse, Retail Space

Now that you have a proper company and bank account, you can pay vendors with the company account for your office, warehouse or retail space (assuming you're not home-based). Some of this work can be done before your company is filed and bank account is open (especially for complex leases or build-outs) but ideally after so you can track expenses in the company properly.

Contacting a commercial real estate broker in your area can be helpful. Make sure to arrange for utilities and office furniture. Also, remember that home office expenses can usually be deducted, so keep careful track of your spending on home offices and supplies.

Obtain Licenses and Permits

Forming the company is the first step. Now, you typically will need to get a license or permit to operate in your local jurisdiction (and sometimes at the federal level) as well as register for various local taxes. The easiest way to determine what you need is to call the local government office where you will operate and ask; they'll typically provide some kind of checklist. If you live within a city you would call city hall; if you live outside the city, then call your county government and ask for the business license division.

If you will be opening a retail location or renting office space, it's important you clear the location for zoning and other issues by contacting the government before signing any lease or other documents.

Federal Permits: Most businesses do not require a federal license or permit. However, if you are engaged in one of the following activities, you should contact the responsible federal agency to determine the requirements for doing business:

- Investment advising (http://www.sec.gov)
- Drug manufacturing (http://www.fda.gov)
- Preparation of meat products (http://www.fda.gov)
- Broadcasting (http://www.fcc.gov)
- Ground transportation (http://www.dot.gov)
- Selling alcohol, tobacco, or firearms (http://www.atf.gov)

State Licenses: Some occupations and professions require a state license or permit. Laws vary from state to state, however, if you are engaged in one of the following professions, you should contact the responsible state agency to determine the requirements for your business:

Tip: Most people engaged in the types of business that require a special state license or permit are already aware of the requirements (e.g. an accountant is familiar with the licensing requirements for accountants).

- accountants
- appraisers
- auctioneers
- banks
- barbers
- bill collectors
- building contractors
- cosmetologists
- funeral directors
- insurance carriers
- physicians
- private investigators
- private security guards
- real estate agents

State Licenses and Permits (based on products sold): Some state licensing requirements are based on the product sold. Contact your state licensing authorities to determine the licensing requirements of your business. For example, most states require special licenses to sell:

- firearms
- food
- gasoline
- liquor
- lottery tickets
- marijuana

Sales Tax Permit: If your company sells physical products, you may have to collect and pay sales tax. This is usually accomplished by obtaining a state seller's permit or resale permit. You can usually register or find the forms online.

Tip: Many service businesses that do not sell a physical, tangible product are not required to collect sales tax, so ask your state taxation agency for details/clarification.

Business License: Most cities or counties require you to obtain a business license, even if you operate a home-based business. This is a license granting the company the authority to do business in that city or county. You can usually find the forms online.

Hire Employees (if applicable)

If you intend to hire yourself (typically required if you are set up as a corporation) or others as a full or part-time employee of your company, then you will have to register with the appropriate state agencies to obtain workers compensation insurance or unemployment insurance (or both).

Employee payroll and laws are so complex that I always recommend people use one of the many payroll services that can be found online (see the Chapter Resources). Not only will they help you register your business properly to hire employees, but they will calculate payroll, pay appropriate taxes, file quarterly forms, track vacation/sick time, and more for as little as $10/month or less per employee. Trust me, it's silly to even consider doing payroll yourself in this day and age. I guarantee it's not worth your time or the risk.

Set up an Accounting and Record-Keeping System

Set up your accounting and record-keeping system and learn about the taxes your new company is responsible for paying.

Accounting is important, not only for tax purposes, but for you to know your cash position, profit and loss and more.

If you initially only have a handful of transactions per month, then you can probably handle bookkeeping yourself at first. Eventually, when it becomes more complex, I recommend you use one of the many online accounting programs and hire a bookkeeper, accountant, or CPA to manage your books (unless this is already a skill you have). Recently, there are online services that will actually do your books (including receiving receipts, invoices via email/scan), reconcile your accounts, provide reports, and even provide access to a CPA for advice for a very low monthly rate that is based on your number of transactions (or similar, see the Chapter Resources). Regardless of how you do it, it's critical that you reconcile your books monthly so you can stay on top of your finances especially in the critical startup phase.

You'll want to maintain a list of all owners and addresses, copies of all formation documents, financial statements, annual reports, amendments, or changes to the company. All tax and corporate filings should be kept for at least three years. Scan and keep everything just in case.

Obtain Business Insurance

There are many types of insurance for businesses, but they are usually packaged as "general business insurance" or a "Business Owner's Policy." This can cover everything from product liability to company vehicles. A decent policy can run as little as $300/year and offers a great extra level of protection and can help you sleep easier at night.

If you provide advice or a complex service, consider an "Error and Omissions" policy. If you are providing a digital service, they even have policies to protect you against claims of lost data or hacking. I recommend you contact a local insurance agent and discuss your needs with them.

Develop a Business Identity

In Step 2, we discussed picking the name and even colors and fonts. A professionally created logo can make your business look professional and established. After your company has been officially filed, now's the time to consider having a professional create a business identity for your company. This has become very inexpensive over the years and a decent logo package can be purchased for under $100 in many cases. You can then order business cards, letterhead and promotional materials for your business from one of the many online vendors (see the Chapter Resources).

Trademarks

A trademark is a name (or phrase), symbol or design identifying and distinguishing a product from goods and services provided by other companies. Unlike registering your business name with the county or state, a federal Trademark offers you nationwide protection of your mark. Well-known trademarks include the Nike Swoosh, the AT&T blue planet, or the phrase "I'm lovin' it®" from McDonald's.

Filing a Trademark:

- A trademark must be distinctive.
- A trademark must not infringe on existing trademarks.
- First, do a comprehensive search to make sure your name or symbol is distinctive and not already registered. You can do this online at USPTO.gov, but there are other databases to search and proper searching is an art.
- Complete the federal application for a trademark with the U.S. Patent and Trademark Office (USPTO) with the filing fee.

- A trademark attorney at the USPTO will review and either accept the trademark application or reject it and return it for resubmission.

- Once the trademark application is accepted, you may use the ® symbol to identify your trademark as officially registered.

Trademark law is complex, and many applications to the USPTO are rejected. That's why we highly recommend that if you want to file a trademark you have a firm that specializes in trademarks perform a comprehensive search and prepare the application.

Tip: If you are reasonably certain you are the first to use a trademark in the US (you would have already done searches at USPTO.gov, online, etc.) then you can add the ™ symbol to your mark to indicate that you are claiming this as yours. This doesn't require a filing at all but is usually the first step in claiming your mark before you file the official trademark.

Advisors: Accountant and Lawyer

Many of the steps above will be made easier if you start a relationship with a good accountant and lawyer. Now, many startups simply cannot afford these people at this time in their company's life cycle, but I encourage you to search online and use one of the many of the "pay as you go" services that are quick, available almost instantly and reasonably priced. There are also legal plans you can buy for a few hours per month of advice as well as the aforementioned accounting services.

Again, having a local trusted advisor is ideal, but consider these services until you can afford this. Finally, I'm a big fan of a regular legal review and financial review of the company top to bottom: contracts, employee manuals, terms and conditions, overall risk profile, etc. that, depending on your finances and risk tolerance, you may want to consider before launch or later on after you're generating income.

Next Steps

If you've made it this far and have actually pulled the trigger, I want to just take a moment and offer you some congratulations. (If you're not there yet and are still researching, don't despair, we'll get there). A lot of people these days talk about starting a business, the "wantrepreneurs" I've previously mentioned, but you actually put yourself out there and took the risk to start. That's to be admired, and, as I wrote in the introduction to this book, is the greatest source of progress and wealth in the world. In the next few sections of our Six-Step system, we'll go over Growing, Managing and ultimately Systemizing this business we've created.

Onward!

Visit http://www.startupsmadesimple.com for Chapter 7 Resources and to download the Startups Made Simple Startup Checklist.

8
STEP FOUR: GROW IT

"By far the biggest leverage point to increase sales is marketing. Marketing is the master skill of business. No one knows how good your product is until after the sale so the best marketer wins every time. Even being 10% better at marketing can have exponential effects on the bottom line."
—Allan Dib, author of *The 1-Page Marketing Plan*

After you've officially filed your paperwork and you're a real company, job number one now is to grow the business. I put this step before the next step, "Manage it" because, as I've mentioned, you don't want to over-plan and optimize things too much when your true focus now should be getting sales and customer feedback so you can improve your product or service. Eventually, the Grow it, Manage it and Systemize it steps work together as you scale your business to your liking.

Generally, there are three ways to grow a business:

- Acquire new customers organically
- Increase sales to existing customers (get them to buy more, buy more frequently or both)
- Encourage existing customers to refer people to your business

A well-designed marketing plan and sales process will help you do all of this and ideally will systemize this it into a replicable Sales Machine that brings you continuous business.

Beware though, if there's one area of business that suffers from confusion and purposeful over-complication (especially by those who sell marketing services) it's marketing and sales. In fact, most small business owners I encounter don't know a lot about marketing and sales and believe the eternal myth "build it and they will come" or think that doing sales is "uncool." So let's start off with clear definitions, then we can move on to strategy and then tactics.

What is Marketing?

Basically, marketing is identifying, then finding or attracting your ideal customer and getting them to trust you (so they buy from you). That's it; that's your marketing strategy. Almost everything you will hear or read related to marketing and sales is simply a tactic of that. Tactics include advertising, writing content, direct mail, public relations and many more that we will go over later in this chapter.

Knowing that marketing includes identifying your ideal customer, that is the first step of your marketing strategy. We've done a lot of this in Steps 1 and 2 of this book (review them if necessary), but now it's time to really get specific and actually make a Simple Marketing Plan that will keep you focused as you grow your business.

What is Sales?

Marketing makes your ideal customer (also known as a "lead") aware of your solution. Sales is the art of demonstrating to your leads that your solution is the best for their needs. Sales is everything your company does to "close the sale", sell the product or get a signed agreement or contract.

Again, almost everything you've heard about sales is probably a tactic. The sales process often includes interpersonal interaction and is often done via one-on-one meetings (sometimes via Internet), cold calls, networking or via your company's brochures or website. Sales is not uncool, it's simply seeing if your product or service is a fit for a potential customer.

Biggest Marketing and Sales Mistakes

As discussed in other chapters, I believe avoiding mistakes is a big part of success in business (and in life). Here are the biggest marketing and sales mistakes I've seen over the years.

- **No marketing at all**. This may be the "build it and they will come" mentality or simple benign neglect, but a sure path to failure is not doing marketing at all or hoping some one-trick pony like a Yellow Pages ad or a stack of business cards will work.

- **Not knowing your ideal customer**. Treating everyone the same (even jerks and cheapskates), targeting everyone with a heartbeat, or trying to make all of your customers happy by catering to their every demand can strain your resources. It is much better to focus on the best customer (see below).

- **No marketing or sales process**. No marketing process, no sales process or plan. Hoping that the phone will ring or people will find them online. Uses lots of Post-It notes, randomly sent emails with or without follow-up. No testing what works, no game plan at all.

- **No response or follow-up**. I've spent tens of thousands of dollars with a vendor simply because they answered the phone, responded to my request in a timely manner, or followed up later. Was this the best vendor? Who knows? Many times I never got a response from their competitors. A lot of success in life comes from just showing up to the game.

- **Cheap marketing materials**. I cringe when I see a company that has a great product or service have some cheaply made logo, website, storefront, or other materials. Humans are not rational and many times will simply go with the best-looking solution, not necessarily the best. Don't cheap out on marketing materials and design.

- **Not focusing on the product or service**. As discussed below, building a great product or service makes your life easier because customers will tell their friends and you'll be much more enthusiastic about marketing and selling something you're proud of and are passionate about.

- **Not knowing why you're better**. If you can't explain (in-person and via your marketing and sales process) why your product or service is better than your competitors (usually in one sentence) then how are your prospects going to know? Read below for more help with this.

- **Not putting one person in charge of marketing**. If you don't have one person in charge of your company's growth then nobody will be in charge. Make one person accountable for growth and have them working on measurable goals.

- **Not knowing the numbers**. As I'll discuss later in the chapter, knowing how much it costs for you to acquire a customer as well as their lifetime value is incredibly valuable.

The Startups Made Simple Marketing Plan

Now that you know the basics of marketing and sales and the biggest mistakes, it's time to make a very simple one-page plan that will guide you and simplify your marketing and sales process. Many of the best companies have a very simple, replicable marketing and sales process that has served them well, sometimes for decades.

Figuring out your ideal market and systemizing how you turn them into customers is one of the biggest secrets to success in business. Your purpose with the Simple Marketing Plan is to initially identify who your ideal customer is by talking to them and getting lots of feedback in the startup phase. Then, you can continue to tweak your product or service to meet their needs or potentially find other markets you may not have been aware of when planning your business.

Start With Your Product or Service

If there's one thing that will make your marketing and sales efforts dramatically easier and more effective, it is simply building a superior product or service: better, cheaper, or faster/easier. There is such a thing as a product or service that's so good that it lives by referrals alone. This is rare, but it does happen, and when it does, you will almost guarantee success. As I mentioned in the Founder Superpowers section, product obsession is a valuable mindset to have.

One thing you may want to focus on is which two of the three features you want in the Product Triangle: the best, the cheapest, or the fastest/easiest. Note that almost no product or service can be all three; you should pick one to focus on and do the best you can with the other two. For example, you can make the best product in the world, but it certainly won't be the cheapest. You can make the cheapest product in the world, but it probably won't be the best. There are trade offs like this, and you should know which you are willing to make.

Once your product or service has been demonstrated to be superior in at least one of those areas, that's where you focus on making what's called a Unique Sales Proposition (USP). Below, you'll target your ideal customer, and one thing to remember when you write your marketing and sales messages is that you need to demonstrate why your product is superior.

Think 80/20 and Think Big

One of the big secrets in business is that 20% of your clients will typically make up 80% of your profits. This is based on what's known as the Pareto Principle in statistics and has proven consistent for centuries across business and life in general (20% of criminals cause 80% of crime, etc.). Similarly, 20% of your products make up 80% of your sales as well. In the startup phase you may not know which clients or products are your most profitable yet, but it's important to starting thinking 80/20 as you grow your business.

So, in your marketing plan, an important step will be identifying your ideal customer and even making a "persona" of this person so you can more easily identify others like them. Begin looking for these 80/20 customers, and remember things like how easy they are to deal with (nobody wants a profitable jerk as a customer), how demanding they are for support, how quickly they pay, and other factors.

A great way to generate innovative marketing ideas is to really stretch your imagination. What if you had a gun to your head and needed to increase sales 10X in one year? What if you had to meet your BHAG® in 6 months? What things would you need to experiment and implement on right now to get this done. Thinking like this is valuable because it lights the fire of motivation and expands your thinking.

Identify Your Ideal Customer

As mentioned, knowing specifically who your ideal customer is, whether they're a person or a business, is the obvious first step in any marketing plan. Once you know who your ideal customer is, then marketing simply becomes a matter of targeting these businesses or people "until they buy or die" as some (hilariously) say.

Identifying your ideal customer is sometimes completely obvious or can be somewhat tricky; especially if you're introducing a new product or service. Many times, this is a process of talking to lots of customers and finding out which type is not only the best match for your product or service, but which type is the most profitable for you and the type you like serving best. Remember, businesses are simply made of people, so in reality, you're likely targeting a specific person in a company (for example, the operations manager or the human resources manager), even if you think you're only selling to businesses.

Identify Personas

Getting to know this person, how they think, what their problems are, what their fears are, and what they care about is the first step in identifying your ideal customer. What keeps them up at night? What do they worry about? Who are they trying to impress or what is the main problem they want to solve? What keywords do they search online to solve their problem? Where do they hang out offline and online?

This is called a "persona," and is extremely effective in clarifying your marketing efforts. Once you know this, then you can build your list of potential prospects and then identify the optimal way to reach these people and inform them of your solution. You will then craft your marketing message to solve this person's problems.

For example, you could be selling consulting services, and after you've worked with a few clients, you begin to discover that a certain type of company is your absolute best client. They're a pleasure to work with, they pay premium rates on time, etc. This could be a certain industry, a certain size company, a certain location, a certain set of problems, or even a certain personality type from the CEO or even the office manager. As you get better at this, you'll be able to laser target these people and your message.

Let's say that the ideal customer in this case is a small manufacturing company in the southwest USA with 20–100 employees and a CEO who is between 40 and 50 years old, forward-thinking but concerned by outsourcing and labor issues like workers compensation expenses. Now our job is much easier. Instead of the 5 million or so businesses in the USA with employees, we now can focus on perhaps just a few thousand or less and craft a marketing message perfectly tailored for their problems and your solutions. This is powerful targeting—instead of millions of targets you have only a few—and now you can spend much more time and money per lead versus an untargeted campaign.

Some businesses never need more than one persona, but many times you may have multiple personas you'd like to target. My recommendation in this startup phase is just to get the biggest and most profitable persona right first, then carefully add others later if necessary.

The startup phase is a learning phase, and it's critical that you find your ideal customer, but keep in mind this process may take a while. You may need to spend many months interviewing leads and customers to find out which one is ideal and to develop the persona. That's why it's so important that once you launch your business that you talk to as many customers and potential customers as possible. This can be as simple as emailing your customer and asking them why they chose you and what convinced them to buy (or asking them in person or phone if possible). A good question I've learned to ask over the years is "What almost prevented you from buying?" to identify possible issues with your marketing or sales process. If you can get important demographic information on them, even better (age, income, location, sex, etc.).

Build Your List

Once you have a decent idea of your ideal customer and their persona, you can begin building your list. It's amazing how powerful this concept can be; you can build one list and continue to attract or reach out to this list systematically.

There are an enormous amount of information resources online for finding businesses and individuals, and I will list several in the Chapter Resources. Depending on your market, you may be able to buy a list, build your own list, or hire a service or assistant to compile the list for you. The main point is that you want to have a good idea who your ideal customer is, begin building your list and start testing out marketing messages.

Test Your Message and Medium

Instead of using a shotgun approach like buying an expensive TV or radio advertisement and then hoping and praying it works, you can run very small tests by targeting your ideal customer with inexpensive tactics. This includes cold calls, cold email, online search engine ads, direct mail (even letters you write yourself), brochures and in-person visits, depending on your market. Once you figure out what works, you can then go all-in and spend many more resources on that proven medium. This has been called "firing bullets before cannonballs" by the business guru Jim Collins.

If you've done the testing work from Step 2, then you may already have a very good idea of your market and perhaps even a message that works. The important thing in this step is to appeal to the persona you are targeting.

There are various ways to do this, including writing ads, websites, blog posts, brochures, white papers, or "special reports" that identify problems they may have and how your product or service solves them. The Chapter Resources lists many more. A good rule of thumb is to spend 5–10% of your marketing budget on experiments each month so you can figure out which medium works best for you.

Writing ads and "copy" is an art itself, so you may consider hiring a pro to write ads for you if you're not good at this yourself. This can involve things like coming up with taglines, headlines, experimenting with images, colors, buttons, etc. and can get pretty involved. Taglines are powerful ways to differentiate yourself from the competition or quickly show why your solution is better in one sentence. See the Chapter Resources for recommendations.

The important thing to know is that when using the above methods you can either "go to them" (outbound marketing) and contact leads directly via an outreach program, or you can create content that makes the lead "come to you" (inbound marketing). Imagine if you could simply make a website that has such valuable content that your leads actively search for you online and contact you. This is what many marketers focus on these days. You attract your ideal lead by providing information and solutions, and answering their questions so well that they immediately find you, trust you, and will purchase your products or services.

Build Your Sales Process

Once you know how to to find your ideal customer and make them aware of your product or service, then it's time to figure out the optimal way to turn this lead into a customer. This will be your sales process, and if you can learn how to replicate it consistently, then there's no limit to how you can grow your company.

Think about it; if you can make a documented, clear sales process that works every time, then you can likely train someone else to do it, which frees you up to do other things—or nothing at all! This is why many companies typically assign regions, states, or even zip codes to salespeople: they have a proven sales process and simply train people to use it — it's like printing money.

The important thing will be to first build your sales process through experimentation. Then, you'll document and streamline it down to the bare basics. You'll know exactly what scripts, copy, ads, and other specifics work to complete a sale.

Modern marketers call this a "sales funnel," and it includes a clear, documented process from beginning (known as the "top" of the sales funnel) to end that can include things like setting an appointment, doing a demo of your product or service, giving a presentation, signing a contract, or making an online purchase. The important thing is to experiment until you know what works.

Elements of a Great Sales Process

1. **Consistent lead generation**. Your marketing efforts provide a consistent source of leads to enter your sales funnel or are otherwise captured for follow-up.

2. **Quick response times**. This varies by industry, but the faster you respond to a lead, the more likely the sale; the best is in-person, live chat or phone. Some industries have shown that same day follow-up to leads dramatically increases sales even versus the next day. Strike while the iron is hot.

3. **Awesome marketing materials: demo, proposal, website, etc**. However you will "sell" your client and what materials you use will vary dramatically by industry. Whatever it is, make sure that it's professional, impressive, comprehensive (answers all their questions), and has lots of social proof (verified testimonials from other customers). Do not skimp on marketing materials.

4. **Great salespeople**. Few things in business are as nice as dealing with a friendly, non-pushy, knowledgeable, competent, and well-spoken salesperson who actually consults with you. Great salespeople are worth their weight in gold and can explode the growth of your company, so make sure you take care of them. See the next section for more.

5. **Consistent follow-up**. The best sales process will have a way to capture the lead and follow up consistently until they buy or express no interest. Sticky notes and emails

are not a "system" in this regard. A good customer relationship management (CRM) system or even a spreadsheet is better.

6. **Great product.** This should already be assumed, but in case I wasn't clear in previous chapters, a great product should be a primary focus and will generate plenty of marketing on its own through word of mouth.

7. **Great after-sales support.** If you provide great support, your customers will keep buying from you, will be more likely to buy more (or upgrade their service), and more likely to refer their friends. Don't look at support as a cost-center, look at it as an opportunity to wow your customer and grow your business.

8. **Ask for feedback and a referral.** You should ask all customers for feedback on their buying experience, which provides a lot of good data for improvements. Happy customers will be happy to give a referral. Build referrals into your sales process by asking customers to refer a friend or even financially reward them for doing so.

Build Your Sales Skills

Take a quick look through any bookstore (or Amazon.com) and you will see thousands of books on sales tactics, skills and more. I have a few recommendations in the Chapter Resources, but as usual, sales is not nearly as hard as many would have you think. It's important to build your sales skills or at least know great sales skills when you see them so you can hire great salespeople.

Overall, sales, like marketing, is about building trust. You build trust by following the Elements of a Great Sales Process above, but also by simply doing what you promise your product or service does. A major element of becoming a great salesperson is building a great product or service that you are proud of, a product or service that you get excited about selling to other people because you know it will solve their problem or improve their life. There are few things more demoralizing than trying to sell a bad product.

Elements of Great Salespeople

1. **They don't sell, they solve problems.** Great salespeople many times don't consider themselves salespeople at all; they're people who educate, consult and advise people who need solutions—they solve problems. This is a great mindset to have if you are hesitant to cold-call people.

2. **They're modest.** Yes, believe it or not, the best people are not like those you see on TV and movies. 91% of top salespeople rate high in modesty and humility. Think about a great salesperson you've encountered; they're probably not egotistical or pushy, and you probably didn't consider them salesy at all or even know they were a salesperson.

3. **They listen.** Nothing is more frustrating than someone who filibusters the conversation or won't let you get a word in edgewise. Great salespeople listen to the real problems and concerns of their prospective customers.

4. **They ask questions.** Known as the Socratic method of selling, great salespeople ask great questions of people, are genuinely curious and can effectively guide the prospect to see if the product they're selling is the right solution for them.

5. **They're competitive.** It's rare to see a great salesperson who doesn't like to compete, to meet and exceed goals and to win whatever game they're playing. If you're not competitive, make sure you hire someone who is.

6. **They don't give up.** Sometimes sales can be demoralizing to a sensitive person, and there are products that less than 1% of the people you contact will want (and the other 99% might not be so nice about telling you they're not interested).

It takes a certain level of skill and an inability to be upset by rejection to overcome the tendency to give up.

7. **They keep their word**. Ever bought something and were completely underwhelmed by the product compared to what the salesperson promised? Of course you have, this is common, and good luck getting a hold of that salesperson again; they're on to the next sucker. Great salespeople provide great "after purchase" support and keep the promises they made during the sales process.

8. **They know the basics**. By now, the basics of Dale Carnegie and other sales training is pretty common knowledge: Remember and use the person's name, proper handshake, eye contact, good personal appearance, return calls/emails quickly, smile, friendly voice, persuasion skills and overall treat people how you'd like to be treated. There's a lot online about this stuff.

Learn the Numbers

After you've started building out your marketing and sales process, you'll soon learn what it costs to get a lead and make a sale. Marketing can become pretty simple after you know these numbers. This is known as your customer acquisition cost (CAC) and is a very valuable number to know.

Think about it, if you can consistently know how much it costs to acquire a new customer, then you can know what it will take to grow your business. You'll also know if you need to raise prices or otherwise pursue a different tactic (perhaps the product simply isn't profitable given the CAC). For example, if you spent $1000 to get ten customers or purchases, you would know that your CAC is $100. A related concept is your conversion rate: if you can convert 1 out of 10 leads into a customer, then your conversion rate is 10%.

Another valuable number to know is the lifetime value (LTV) of a customer. How much does the typical customer spend throughout their time as your customer? This can be measured over months or years and may not be known yet in the startup phase. The LTV is very valuable because if you know the CAC and the LTV, then you know, almost exactly, how much you can afford to spend on your marketing and sales efforts.

For example, let's say I sell a product for on average $100; this is known as your "average ticket." If I do the numbers and figure out that my CAC is $100 per new customer, I may think that this is unprofitable (I made $0 on their first purchase), and I need to go back to the drawing board or try something else.

However, if I know that over their lifetime (LTV) they'll spend $400 with me on average, then I know, depending on time frame (let's assume one year), that I can actually afford to spend much *more* than $100 acquiring this customer and still be profitable. Once you know the numbers, you may find out that even something that doesn't seem profitable is actually very profitable to you.

Pivot If Necessary

The final thing I'll mention is that sometimes you will find that through all of your efforts the marketing is not effective and the sales are not coming in as you'd like. Remember that we talked about perseverance in the Founder Superpowers; it's not considered quitting if the market fires you. Sometimes a product or service simply will not sell.

In these cases, depending on many factors, make sure you exhaust all options before you go back to the drawing board. Here are some things to consider if the product is not selling:

1. **Talk to customers**. Make sure you're talking to your customers. Send them an email or give them a call (or speak to them in person if possible). They'll tell you what the problem is and will be happy to do so.
2. **Raise or lower prices**. You should have a sense of your CAC and LTV as mentioned earlier. Sometimes lowering

prices can increase volume considerably. Or sometimes raising prices can increase sales as well (and make more per customer). People and prices are not rational, so it's important to experiment with pricing. Most people start out charging too little.

3. **Brainstorm alternatives**. Make a list of everything else you can do with this product or service as it is or with minimal tweaking to make customers happy. For example, can you add consulting to your product? Can you sell it to a competitor? Can you give it away for free and sell a service with it? Can you split, combine, resell, or otherwise modify it? Make a list of these alternatives and keep talking to customers.

4. **Use the system**. Go back to Steps 1 and 2 to reimagine and test things if necessary. Remember that a pivot is completely normal and some of the biggest success stories have done it, sometimes many times.

Onward!

Visit http://www.startupsmadesimple.com for Chapter 8 Resources and to download the Startups Made Simple Marketing Plan.

9
STEP FIVE: MANAGE IT

"Management is doing things right; leadership is doing the right things." —Peter F. Drucker

Once you've figured out how to make at least "ramen money" and sales start rolling in, things may start to get a bit chaotic simply because of all the moving parts (many of which will be newly invented or made up on the fly,) and if you are new to startups, this may be challenging. Remember, you need to grow this machine, but this is where things can get complex, so try to keep them simple. Your goal should be growing sales while minimizing or even eliminating complexity.

Most startups and small businesses are notoriously poorly managed, almost a joke. If you do the basics here, then you'll be well ahead of the game with, again, just a few hours of planning. The purpose of this chapter is to provide a framework for some order and direction in your company so you can navigate the complexity of what will likely be an almost constantly changing environment and create your management system. If you already have a company that needs a better management system, then this chapter (and the next) will help as well.

I want to emphasize that your focus will likely be making sales at this point and *not* optimizing the management of things prematurely. There's little purpose in optimizing a business with few or no sales (unless you have plenty of time or are planning for an expected sales explosion). However, there's no harm in getting the basics of small business management down and being prepared for the moment when you need to start scaling things. Certainly it is better to organize things before the company's growth and complexity get out of control.

While I do recommend some basic planning which will save you a ton of time later, one thing I tell founders, especially types who are very well organized, there is going to be some chaos, waste and inefficiencies at first. This is all very natural in a startup, so please don't think you can organize all this chaos all the time. Just keep a list of things you need to fix and revisit them when you can.

Do the best you can and get a "nicely managed chaos" going until you have the time to set up some proper systems. Keep the Founder Superpowers in mind, get the big things done, and make sure that you schedule time to work on building your management system. The purpose of the next chapter, Step 6: Systemize it, is to bring everything we go over in this chapter together in a beautifully well-run system (and what I call "The Manual") but realize that may take a while as you figure out and build out all the working parts.

For example, once you start making sales you may have no organized invoicing or sales process. You might find that you need to make a hire and have no idea where to start or your existing hires are not doing well. Or you may start to notice that things in customer service are starting to get sloppy or confused, and you feel you need to write things down to stay organized.

Whatever the trigger, there are some pretty simple and clear solutions to a lot of this chaos, and I put them in these five categories that I call **The Five Competencies**:

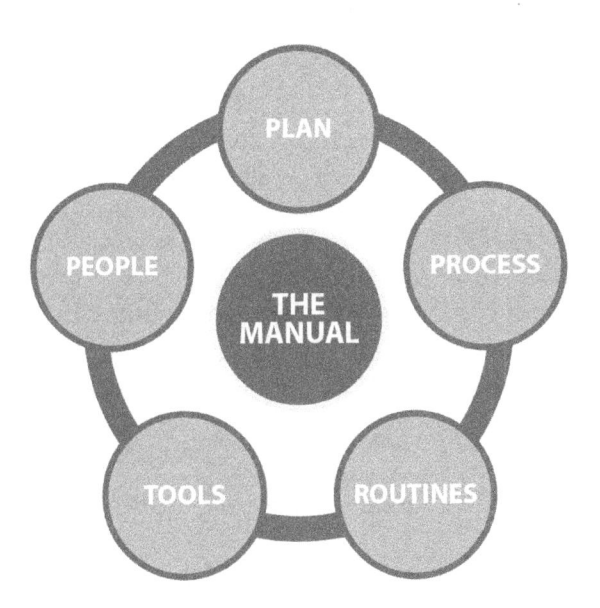

(Diagram: Five circles arranged around a central circle labeled "THE MANUAL". The surrounding circles are labeled PLAN, PROCESS, ROUTINES, TOOLS, and PEOPLE.)

1. **The Right Plan.** You'll make a simple one-page plan so that you and everyone else knows the company purpose, strategy, and goals, and are aligned and rowing in the same direction. This will not only clarify your thinking but also give much-needed direction to your team because many employees have no idea what the company purpose or strategy is or how they fit in it.

2. **The Right Process.** A business is mostly just a system of process and procedures that delivers an end result (the product or service). These procedures can be listed, organized by function, assigned an accountable person, optimized, and documented into simple, repeatable, easily-trainable written procedures. This is critical to systemizing your company and ultimately gaining freedom from chaos and being stuck in day-to-day management.

3. **The Right People**. The key to making everything work is hiring and training the right people. Most small businesses are terrible at this, and I will show you how to greatly improve your business with some simple hiring, training, and performance management best practices that work.

4. **The Right Tools**. The tools and systems you need to create or acquire to solve problems, make everything work together, and further streamline how you work.

5. **The Right Routines**. The regular meetings to solve problems and improve your strategy, process, people, and tools. The work routines you need to master to continuously deliver excellent service to your customers. Routines prevent entropy in your organization and keep everything aligned.

Here are some ground rules for working on your management system:

- If you're starting up, write things down or otherwise organize things in a central place (the same document or folders) and clean them up based on the structure I provide. For example, as you learn new procedures like invoicing or running payroll, write things down and centralize your information (or if it's a manual, print it out and put in a folder, or my preferred method: scan documents into a digital folder), put it all in the same place for "Procedures" for easy reference and organize it as you go.

- Focus on one of The Five Competencies at a time if possible, usually the one that needs the most improvement first. If you're just starting out, focus on The Right Plan.

- If you have an existing company that needs to be cleaned up, focus on one of the areas per week or even per month and make sure your team understands and "buys in" to the value in making things easier for everyone (including themselves and your customers). If you try to do all these things at once and without team buy-in, then you will have a hard time and only frustrate people.

- Remember that creating your management system is extremely valuable work and will ultimately lead to your freedom.

The Right Plan

"Strategy is not a lengthy action plan. It is the evolution of a central idea through continually changing circumstances." —Jack Welch

It's hard to overstate how important having a simple, clear strategic plan is, not only for your clarity of mind, but to get your team to understand where the company is supposed to go. Most small businesses have no clear strategy or goals besides the whim of the founder at that time. The founder may have a vision with no clear goals or action items, which will get you nowhere fast. Some founders have plenty of goals with no vision to guide them, which can actually be counterproductive ("chasing squirrels").

The Founder Superpowers section of this book provides plenty of guidance on vision and execution, but the guiding light should be a simple one-page plan that organizes everything in one place and shows your team exactly where the company is going and what needs to get done.

Elements of the Right Plan

You may not know some of these elements if you're still trying to figure out your product, haven't hired staff yet, or haven't generated much revenue. The point is that it's important to get a first version of the plan. It will always be a work in progress and needs to be known by everyone, reviewed and updated frequently as your company grows and changes, which we'll go over when we discuss The Right Routines.

- **Vision.** As discussed in chapters 2, 5 and 6, a clear vision that is well communicated puts the same picture in everyone's head and can be extremely motivational and clarifying. This lets everyone know the future they're working towards every day.

- **Purpose.** Answer this question: Why do you wake up every day and work toward your vision? Who are you serving? Knowing your "why" is incredibly motivational if it inspires you to action.

- **Values and principles.** What do you value and what do you stand for? Knowing this will help you differentiate between good and bad decisions. There's more on this in Step 6.

- **One-sentence strategy.** Closely related to the elevator pitch in Step 2, the one-sentence strategy is an easily-remembered, easily-communicated, broad summary of how you're going to reach your vision.

- **Goals.** Vision and purpose are great, but you need to have concrete, measurable goals, that you work toward, perhaps even a BHAG® as described in chapter 2. Definitely, you want goals for the year (broken down by quarter), and many great companies have 3, 5 or even 10-year goals for things like product, revenue, profit, etc. See chapter 2 for a summary of goals and how to break them down.

- **Scoreboard.** Can I glance at the plan and know how we're doing? A well-designed scoreboard (sometimes an electronic dashboard or even manually collected stats) will measure a handful of metrics (revenue, profit, number of leads, etc.) and let you know the status of your goals (usually green, yellow, or red).

Take the time to create your first plan and get it in front of your whole team then refer to it and keep improving it forever. You'll be amazed how this simple one-page document can radically clarify what needs to get done and simplify how you operate your business. The Chapter Resources has a sample version for you to use.

The Right Process

If there is a key to small business freedom (in addition to having enough sales to live comfortably), it's getting control of and mastery over the processes and procedures inside your company. Every business is simply a collection of activities, most of which can be identified and documented. Once documented, it can be simplified and taught to others.

Having others (either employees or contractors) take over working procedures is how you stop working *in* your business and start working *on* (improving) your business. Procedures free up your time to work on strategy, growing and systemizing your business further. The rich get richer because of this cycle; they delegate the little things and focus exclusively on the big things that generate huge returns. They then delegate the implementation of those bigger things and repeat.

When I first started my company in 2001, there was very little information on how to properly structure process in a company (outside of some internal documents for very large companies). There was *The E-Myth* by Michael Gerber and some vague references in other books and articles, but nothing that showed exactly what I needed to do. I was hopelessly lost and overwhelmed. Now, there's not only a lot of information online about "standard operating procedures (SOPs) but several good books and even software that will make systemizing your procedures much easier (which I will reference in the Chapter Resources).

How to Get the Right Process

First, some quick definitions:

- System: a set of principles or procedures to get a result
- Process: a series of actions or steps taken in order to achieve a particular result
- Procedure: step-by-step instructions for doing a process or part of a process
- Policy: a system of principles to guide decisions

You will probably have about 5–10 big processes in your business, for example, your marketing process, your hiring and training process, or your customer service process. Then, within each process, you will have specific step-by-step procedures. For example, within the marketing process, you may have "Writing a Blog Post" or "Managing our Google Adwords Account" as written procedures. Finally, you'll have various policies dealing with things like employee time off, safety, customer service and more.

Over the years, these are the steps and best practices I've learned to get process right in a business.

1. **List the procedures**. Make a list of every *recurring* procedure that you do to run your business (daily, monthly, quarterly, yearly, etc.). You might want to track things for a few weeks and list them as you do them, including such tasks as invoicing clients, paying bills, paying taxes, ordering office supplies, customer support, maintaining machines, managing marketing activities (blogging, managing advertising accounts, etc.), and everything that you do to serve your customers, which will vary dramatically from business to business.

2. **Group the procedures**. You will see that many procedures are closely related as a process and will probably fall into the categories of Admin (everything your company

manages internally like paying bills, ordering supplies, payroll, taxes, hiring, etc.), Operations (everything your company does to deliver your product or service to your customers including providing customer service), and Marketing/Sales (everything your company does to identify, attract and convert leads into sales), or some other similar grouping (Operations may be split between Operations and Customer Service, for example). It's up to you if you want to have these as formal departments at this point and note that some processes go across departments (for example, hiring and training).

3. **Assign an accountable person**. This may only be you for now, but if you have staff and they generally manage a group of procedures, then assign them as the accountable person who is now in charge of these procedures. Make sure to have a good talk with them about why you're doing this and what you're trying to accomplish (and review Superpower #14: Accountability Mindset). Let them know you want their help in getting procedures documented in the company and how valuable it is (and will make their life easier as well). If you're looking to hire, include documenting procedures as one of their initial responsibilities.

4. **Write the procedures**. Either write or have your accountable person write the procedures one by one. See the Chapter Resources for an example of a Written Procedure (including proper naming).

    a. Start by writing the procedure that is the most burdensome or gives you or your team the most grief. Putting things down in writing will help clarify your thinking so you can simplify it.

    b. I highly recommend you start with digital documents at first (so you can move, copy/paste/edit them later) but paper documents will do if that's all you have.

c. Don't overthink and just try to get as much of the basics you can down. Aim for 80% or higher but don't kill yourself getting to 100%. A good goal is to have the procedure detailed enough so that someone new can get the basics with some quick training.

d. If your procedures are complex or you or your staff are having a hard time writing them, make a Procedure for Procedures that shows exactly how to write them for your company step-by-step.

e. Don't bother writing rarely done procedures right now; focus on the recurring procedures. A good way to prioritize is to start with the harder procedures you do daily, weekly, monthly, quarterly, and then yearly.

5. **Review the procedures**. Go over each procedure with your team to make sure they are generally correct and "how we do it." You'll have time later to optimize and streamline, but for now, take a quick glance and identify any "this doesn't make sense" steps or missing steps. Edit them and make final versions for publishing or storage.

6. **Centralize the procedures**. Determine whether you're going to use a binder or store them digitally (or both). It's important that you centralize all of them so they are easily accessible and updatable by your team. I prefer an intranet or shared drive (printing updates to binders can be a hassle). Make sure they're listed in some kind of order somewhere (either a table of contents or a spreadsheet) and reference them by number if appropriate (1.1, 1.2, for one department, 2.1, 2.2 for another, etc.). We'll discuss this more in The Right Tools.

7. **Schedule the procedures**. You will have procedures that are daily, weekly, quarterly, etc. Figure out how best to track that they are getting done using a spreadsheet, a calendar or specialized software I recommend in the Chapter Resources.

8. **Use and maintain the procedures.** You have to actually use the procedures and keep them maintained for them to be effective. Make sure all staff are aware of their location and that the accountable person is responsible for monitoring and keeping them updated. There should be a simple system for requesting an update, writing the update, notifying people of the update and recording when it was last updated (a simple spreadsheet usually works).

9. **Optimize the process and procedures.** Once you have them listed and documented, you can now look at your processes and procedures holistically and identify duplication, constraints, bottlenecks, inefficiencies and find ways to streamline or even eliminate steps. The whole point is to get everything so simple that anyone can take over any process or procedure with little training. Try to review or optimize a major process every quarter as one of your goals.

Two Processes to Get Right

I think two procedural and policy areas that are important to get right early for a startup are the 1) customer service and 2) money and compliance issues. All the processes and procedures are important, but I want to emphasize these two because getting them right will remove a lot of vulnerability and problems in a fragile startup.

Customer Best Practices

Within your Operations written procedures, you should start documenting how to take proper care of your customers. This will vary from business to business but providing good service is an antidote to complaints, bad reviews, angry clients, angry employees, lawsuits, and generally being miserable all day. You will kill momentum and morale if you have angry customers, so take care of them as best you can from the beginning.

At the very least, manage expectations and provide plenty of self-service information that's easily accessible or provide it with your product or service. Well-written documentation, FAQs, welcome packages, emails, or other helpful information will answer your customers' questions before they ask them. The best service in this regard is no service; the best companies have a system or product where customers rarely or never have to ask for help at all.

Finally, one thing in small business I think is important is to realize that the customer is *not* always right. There are simply some humans who cannot be satisfied, appeased, or even reasoned with, and they will make you and your staff miserable. In these cases, I try to have a manager (or myself) have a conversation with the customer. But if that doesn't work, then don't feel guilty about firing them as a customer, refunding their money if appropriate, and even referring them to a competitor as "more suitable to their needs."

Money and Compliance Best Practices

Money management, compliance and controls are fairly obvious, but a lot of entrepreneurs drop the ball and pay for it dearly. Some of these are in the category of business-ending, so I mention them here as a cautionary note to make sure you pay attention to them.

Money Management Best Practices

These can obviously be a lot more complicated depending on your situation. Most of them are easily resolved with some quick research and basic common sense.

- **Be frugal**. Be frugal and don't get cocky! Big offices, expensive parties, and similar luxuries in the startup phase are some well-known ways to break the bank (and probably jinx yourself). You'll have plenty of time and cash later if you run things well, so don't rush to do the flashy stuff until you can easily afford it and really need it. Note that being frugal is not being cheap; don't cheap out on the important things.

- **Establish controls.** Almost every case of theft, loss or mismanagement of cash in business (by employees or others) has to do with the lack of controls. Be very cautious granting full access to money, bank/credit accounts and expensive inventory (or don't do it at all). Background checks for employees with access is recommended. Video monitoring and other security mechanisms may be necessary for physical locations, inventory, etc.

- **Accounting literacy.** Learn basic accounting. Accounting is just money moving in and out of your business and keeping track of it (and other things like inventory and other assets). Don't over-complicate accounting if the money management part of your business is not core to what you do (example: banking, finance, loans, investing, etc.).

- **Understand financial reports.** Learn to read and understand the three most important accounting reports: the Profit and Loss statement (the P & L, so you can know if you're making money or not), the Balance Sheet, and the Cash Flow statement (especially if you are not pre-paid or paid upfront for your work and have to bill clients), and perhaps others depending on the complexity of your financials. Every good founder has a decent grasp of the numbers.

- **Reconcile monthly.** Reconcile your books at least monthly or make sure your bookkeeper does. This is the only way to know your true numbers regardless of what your bank account says.

- **Keep business and personal separate.** Do not commingle your personal money with the business money. Know how to properly reimburse yourself and others from the company accounts. Know how to properly distribute profits and dividends from the company.

- **Manage receivables**. Don't just send a bill once and hope it gets paid. You want to actively manage receivables with various methods like getting to know the accounts payable person, sending big invoices via FedEx to ensure delivery, putting due dates on invoices (instead of the nebulous "due on receipt" or "Net 30"), following up late payments via phone and email, and consider sending past due accounts to collections.

- **Don't keep all your eggs in one basket**. Be very careful about having one or a handful of customers that make up the bulk of your revenue; any change in the relationship can be devastating to your business. Be especially careful of any billing that goes past 30 days; they can likely afford to pay late but that may be damaging to you if they do. Make sure to run a company's credit before giving them any billing terms.

Compliance

Compliance is pretty broad but basically means anything you can get into legal trouble or trouble with the government. Generally this means making sure to get your legal ducks in a row and pay your taxes on time. A lawyer can do a good legal review of everything if you can afford it but there are some common sense best practices to avoid most issues.

Compliance Best Practices

- **Business entity**. Treat your corporation or LLC as a separate entity, maintain all licenses/permits, file all necessary annual reports, don't commingle cash, document decisions in writing, and follow basic corporate compliance, which means holding meetings and writing minutes. This is how you protect your corporate veil and what protects your personal assets in a lawsuit. For a simple solution to this, visit https://www.mycompanyworks.com/premium

- **Legal landmines.** By far the biggest threats are customer, vendor, and employee lawsuits. Review them below and make sure to review with an attorney anything you believe is not rock-solid. Good insurance can also cover many of these issues as well, so speak to an insurance representative if necessary.

  - **Customer lawsuits.** Frankly, most customer lawsuits are bad situations that simply escalated between the business and customer until someone got mad and called a lawyer. You always want to de-escalate if possible, but don't hesitate to vigorously defend yourself as there are some very sue-happy people out there. A good product or service, good customer service, clearly written terms and conditions (acknowledged by the customer in writing), and a safe and clean office or retail location are good antidotes to lawsuits.

  - **Vendor lawsuits.** These mostly have to do with payment and service issues. These can be more complex as a big vendor can be more aggressive and have more resources than your average consumer. With vendors, you want to be very careful with any legal agreements you sign and review their terms and conditions very carefully (if ordering from them is dependent on accepting them). Don't hesitate to have a lawyer review big agreements and "push back" on items of disagreement (the other party will be used to it and probably surprised if you don't), especially evergreen contracts that renew automatically and anything that limits your ability to act against them for various bad things that might happen.

  - **Employee lawsuits.** Many employee lawsuits are from disgruntled employees, so make sure to hire and manage (and fire) well as shown in The Right People section.

Again, you always want to de-escalate if possible but don't hesitate to vigorously defend yourself as you don't want to provoke others. Make sure to have a clear employee manual and ensure that it is signed and acknowledged by each new employee. Make sure to follow all federal, state, and local hiring laws, especially safety, discrimination and sexual harassment laws. Document absolutely everything in writing to be safe, especially underperformance or behavior problems. Use a payroll service to ensure tax and other compliance issues regarding pay.

- **Contractors vs employees**. Make sure you know the definition of a contractor (someone you hire to perform a specific task or project but do not control their schedule or work methods) and an employee (someone you hire to perform a job but can control their schedule and methods of work). The main difference in paying them is how taxes are taken out for employees. There are stiff IRS penalties for hiring a contractor to do employee work. Check the official IRS definitions for more.

- **Taxes**. This should go without saying, but let me just emphasize how expensive late and underpayment fees can be or how badly an audit or other paperwork nightmare can disrupt your business. Pay your taxes and don't ever try to skirt on them.

- **Security issues**. If you deal with technology or have an office location you'll want to make sure you have a written security policy regarding things like passwords (hard to guess, changed frequently), alarm pass codes, backups of data and any industry specific requirements like Payment Card Industry (PCI) Compliance if you accept credit cards.

Have a systems mindset about your business and keep things in writing. This solves so many problems and makes life so much easier that it astonishes me that most small businesses are so bad at it. Take the time to get the Right Process down.

The Right People

Finding the right people for a small business with limited resources is a challenge to say the least. You probably will be offering limited or no benefits (about ⅓ of small businesses offer zero benefits or even paid time off, less than ½ offer health insurance) and a pretty uncertain future, especially as a startup. Not offering benefits or job security is going to eliminate a lot of people from the potential job pool. I would say that finding and keeping the right people is probably the number one problem in businesses both large and small. There are hundreds of books (and consultants, websites, etc.) on this topic, so hopefully we can simplify this process into the core basics.

I believe the best way to find, train and keep the right people includes:

- **Pay Better and Offer Non-Compensation Benefits**
- **Write Great Job Descriptions and Ads**
- **Good Interviews and Assessments**
- **Train and Onboard Properly**
- **People Management Best Practices**

Pay Better and Offer Non-Compensation Benefits

If you read anything about modern business management, you're likely going to encounter an article on how to motivate millennials or young people in general. I've seen so many of these (and related videos, presentations and more) that I'm starting to wonder if something is in the water to make their generation so different from others. While Generation Xers like myself and older generations tend to laugh and dismiss a lot of that stuff, I believe there are some good points to be made about millennials (who are now the largest part of the workforce) and the modern workplace in general.

Think about it; this generation has inherited massive debt from the previous generations (which makes us look incompetent and selfish), their job prospects are dwindling due to global competition, outsourcing and automation (things mostly done by us), and if they try to improve the situation by going to college, they add on even more debt (and their degree may only get them a job as a barista). Social media (again, mostly invented by their elders) has taken normal human interactions and exposed and complicated them so much that anxiety, depression and various ADHD-like disorders are now rampant and many are hopelessly addicted to their devices.

To add insult to injury, they then have their elders telling them to "just get a job and work hard like I did." As if the modern workplace is anything like the manufacturing job you could get in the 1970s straight out of high school with full benefits, rock-solid job security, a pension, and pay good enough to raise a family of four on a single income. Needless to say, I think we need to give the younger generations a break or at least the benefit of the doubt. I'm not saying that some don't make bad decisions; I'm saying that bad decisions and lack of work ethic are not the whole story.

So what do these modern workers want? Surveys say they tend to care more about having some kind of impact at work while having a good life-work balance. By "impact," they mean they want to contribute, see their work as valuable, and not work for a company that acts like an evil empire (and ideally is doing some good).

By "work-life balance," they mean they don't want to work themselves to death like previous generations (especially when there is so little company loyalty to employees these days) and would like to get some kind of benefits at the job. Notice that I didn't mention high pay. This is consistently a lower priority to them than the things we mentioned; they mostly want *fair* pay and regular performance reviews.

Employers want accountable people that can get the job done, but a lot of employees want things like impact and benefits. As with most things in life, I think we can arrive at a nice balance.

I believe a small business should always pay the most they can afford for the best people possible. I see small business owners consistently offering rock-bottom wages and expecting top-dollar performance. They should know better, and frankly, an extra $1 or $2 per hour is only $40 or $80 per week extra per full-timer, and you'll attract a much higher caliber of employee. Let me just say that the difference between a good employee and a mediocre one is usually worth way more than $40 or $80/week, and this increases exponentially as you go up the talent and pay scale.

However, many times a startup is short on cash or may work in a low-skill or low-margin industry (perhaps with many employees) and the extra $1 or $2 per hour is the difference between a profit and a loss. In these cases, and in general, I think it's important that you offer some sort of non-compensation benefits. Offering these will help employees have a better work-life balance and will generally increase job satisfaction. The best part is they don't cost much and are pretty easy to implement.

Some great non-compensation benefits are:

- **Flex-time.** A lot of managers don't understand how hard it is to get to a doctor's appointment, the bank, or even a child's haircut during working hours. Have a simple policy of "take an hour, make up an hour" and let your employees relax to get these things done without hassle.

- **Simple or no dress code.** Nothing grinds my gears more than a company that requires their employees to dress up when they have zero customer interaction or the customer doesn't care about their appearance. Laundering, dry-cleaning, and applying makeup for a strict dress code adds unnecessary time, expense, and hassle to everyone's life. If it's not absolutely required, do away with formal dress codes or only require them for certain employees (salespeople or retail employees, for example).

- **Work from home options.** If the job can be done from home as effectively as it can in-office, then at least offer to allow some work from home.

- **Meals and snacks.** It's amazing, if you read reviews of companies on some employee review sites, even the horribly dysfunctional companies get praise for providing meals or snacks. Keep a fridge stocked with your employee's favorite beverage or snack and buy your team lunch or dinner when you can.

- **Holidays off.** I realize a lot of businesses are open on holidays (and in fact, even busier on those days) but that doesn't mean that *every* employee has to work *every* holiday; this will just demoralize them. For example, if they have to work on Christmas Eve, make sure they get Christmas Day or New Years Day off.

- **Grieving and/or unpaid time off.** Allowing ample time for grieving and sick care is just common decency. Modern life is complex, and sometimes an employee needs to step away for awhile to deal with various issues. This benefit can be abused but I've found that to be rare.

- **Birthday gifts.** I think it's also common decency to at least acknowledge employees' birthdays, so make sure you have them on a calendar. Cards, gifts, and even letting them take the day off would be great additions as well.

- **Predictable schedule.** If you want to drive a human crazy, then make sure they have no idea when they're working until the last minute, don't give them consecutive days off, and give them zero ability to plan any kind of vacation or personal time. Seriously, at least make their schedule as predictable as possible and get better at scheduling yourself if this is an issue.

- **Good environment**. Nobody likes to go into a dark, depressing, messy office or location. At the bare minimum, keep things clean. Natural light, good air conditioning, and measures to control sound are all good ideas (some repetitive or annoying sounds can drive people crazy). Don't underestimate good sound control or dealing with employees who have loud or otherwise annoying vocal habits.

- **Good tools**. Dealing with old computers, broken machines, out-of-date systems, uncomfortable chairs, and more can just add unnecessary stress to the job and will decrease productivity. Schedule a regular review to assess and update your tools. See the section on The Right Tools.

- **Good management**. Everything in this chapter is about having an effective management system in your company. Clear job descriptions, written procedures, regular reviews, best practices, and effectively dealing with hassles and issues all make work a more pleasant place. The Golden Rule also applies here; treat your team as you'd like to be treated if you were them.

Finally, if you build a great business with great vision, values, execution, and leadership, then you're naturally going to offer your employees a workplace where they feel like their work matters and they can contribute. Paying better, offering some of the benefits above, and building a great management system will all work toward your ability to attract and keep the right people.

Write Great Job Descriptions and Ads

If there's one thing that will immediately improve the quality of your hiring, it is writing great job descriptions. Great job descriptions then become great job ads. Great job ads attract better quality candidates and can actually filter out lower-quality candidates, which will save you a lot of time and grief.

The Job Description

It's important that when you go to hire someone that you've written a clear job description that covers exactly what needs to get done, what the definition of "done" is, and the skills and traits of the ideal person to get that job done. That's basically it; it doesn't have to be that hard, and many job descriptions fit on one page. Here are some quick tips for writing job descriptions:

- **Identify what's needed first.** When you're looking to hire someone, try to make sure you know exactly what's needed and what you're hiring them for. Many founders simply get overwhelmed and hire somebody (anybody) to help them out of desperation. Make a list of tasks that need to get done (see the Right Process section above), and identify the tasks you want to delegate (especially the ones that you hate). Group them into a job or jobs with related functions (Admin, Operations, etc.).

- **Write a narrative.** While the above will be a list, write a paragraph or two of exactly what the mission for this position is, why you're hiring them, and what they're generally expected to do each day. Just writing this out will clarify exactly the type of person you need.

- **Describe the desired results.** Now list the results you expect. This is important for accountability and what you will emphasize in interviewing candidates. You can show them this list and what's expected.

- **Describe the qualification and skills.** What does this person have to be competent at to deliver the desired results? List everything from educational background requirements to personality traits like patience or resourcefulness. Note that a lot of the Founder Superpowers are great traits to hire for and develop in your hires, so look to them for inspiration.

- **Define measurable metrics**. Try to identify 3–5 measurable accountabilities for each job, so that when you have to evaluate their performance, you can point to each measure and see how well they're doing. For example, for a customer service agent or supervisor, it might be the customer satisfaction score in surveys or the number of customer complaints.

There are other tools like the Job Scorecard made famous by the book and hiring system called *Topgrading* by Bradford Smart. But, like other things, it's important to just get down some basics first to organize your thinking and tweak and improve them as you go. Writing good job descriptions will do 90% of the the work in writing job ads, which is what we'll cover next.

The Job Ad

Most job ads are terrible, and then the business owner is surprised when they get terrible applicants. For example, here's a real job ad I randomly pulled off of Craigslist (there are many just like this) for an Office Assistant:

> *Office Assistant needed for real estate office. No real estate experience needed. Part time — 20 hours/week — with potential for full time at a later date. Must be able to use online websites to upload and download information, track deadlines and due dates, use Adobe, and Microsoft office. Please email resume with cover letter for consideration. Hourly pay with no benefits.*

Let's analyze this:

1. As a potential employee, I know absolutely nothing about this company. What does this company do? Do they sell or manage real estate or maybe they invest in real estate? What is the company name? Are they trying to hide something

by not even putting their business name on the ad? How could I do further research on them to see if I'd enjoy working there? What does the company value and what is the work environment like? This could be the greatest or worst company on earth, but how would I know?

2. There's no pay specified at all. Does this pay $9/hour or $20/hour? Who knows, and dozens of applicants will have to guess if this is worth their time, within their range of salary requirements necessary to live and possibly go through a long interview to find out. This is a complete waste of everyone's time. If a business has a fantasy of hiring someone worth $20/hour for $10/hour by not specifying salary, it's just that—a fantasy. Good people know what they're worth.

3. What is required, and what does every day look like? I see a few requirements like Microsoft Office, but what do they really need? Expert-level Excel spreadsheet formulas or just basic Microsoft Word? Adobe what? Photoshop or Acrobat? How many words per minute typing speed should this require? Will I be mostly doing email or on the phones all day? Some people are great at one or the other.

4. They've required nothing specific to filter out poor candidates. They've simply asked to email a resume and cover letter. With so many modern tools for applicants to quickly apply to dozens of job ads in a day, it's important to require something out of the ordinary to filter candidates for your company (provided you've even described your company and the job well). Trust me, you'll want a filter. Our last job opening received over 400 candidates, and ¾ of them were filtered as I'll describe below.

5. They haven't pushed the benefits of the job at all (if there are any) and then say "no benefits" to drive home the misery. Remember our discussion about benefits above? You're not going to get the best candidates if you have nothing to offer them, not even the most meager of things like some flex-time.

Now that I've pummeled that ad to death (sorry, this is a big pet peeve of mine), let's see what a job ad looks like that regularly gets hundreds of well-qualified candidates and has proven to work for years. Note that it's for the exact same title of Office Assistant. Also note that, while it is long, it can be easily shortened to be placed in classified ads with a link to a job website (e.g. company.com/jobs) to view the full description.

Job Opening: Office Assistant

Company Overview: Would you like to work for a small business that has its act together, believes in strong core values, is rated A+ by the Better Business Bureau and has been run profitably and ethically since 2001?

MyCompanyWorks is looking for an energetic, friendly, detail-oriented Office Assistant to work in a fairly busy but positive small-business setting. This job will consist of mostly administrative support tasks (mailing, scanning, sorting, filing, heavy email and document management, etc.), generating documents using our internal system and answering inbound phone calls and chats about incorporation and business filings (we help people start businesses, so we do all the filings to start and maintain a business). You must be willing to learn, have a great attitude, and appreciate our laid-back work environment with no dress code (shorts and flip-flops are okay!). We will fully train for this position.

We are a profitable company that is highly organized and technology-proficient so we expect our employees to be the same. Because of our small size, people who like working for large companies may not be a great fit. We work with entrepreneurs on a daily basis so we value entrepreneurial behavior and problem-solving skills. We value a pleasant work environment so we are not into being overbearing, berating or any of that nasty stuff. We will train you for the position, assist you with any questions you might have and leave you alone to do your job as effectively as possible.

Job Location: 187 E. Warm Springs Rd., Suite B, Las Vegas, NV 89119

Compensation: $13–$15/hour DOE + Bonus

Hours: 40 hours per week, Mon-Fri; 8:00am-4:30pm preferred but are flexible around those hours

Qualifications (What we want):

- A friendly voice and great attitude (it's said "you can't teach friendly," so we *must* hire for that and a great attitude)
- Excellent time management skills (you love calendars and lists, keeping things tidy)
- Fast and efficient processing of documents, mail, packages, scans, and emails
- Supreme attention to detail (small spelling/grammar/style mistakes in our line of business can be costly and time-consuming)
- Punctuality
- **Must complete a skills assessment and pass a background and reference check.**

Disqualifications (What we don't want):

- Impatience or bad attitude
- Poor time management: inability to multitask
- Unreliable
- No phone experience, no desire to be on the phone
- Easily overwhelmed or "thin-skinned"

Duties Include:

- Mail forwarding, sorting, and processing
- Create shipping labels and meter postage
- Scanning/uploading documents
- Preparing legal documents using our internal system
- Heavy document management (computer files, attachments, shared folders, etc.)
- Inbound call screening/routing

- Sending notification emails, follow-ups, forwarding mail using our internal system
- Preparing folders, inventory, and ordering office supplies, etc.
- Answer basic questions about our company and service; provide basic support to existing clients
- Other duties or special projects as assigned

Experience:

- Typing skills, more than 50 WPM required (we will test for this)
- Pass our internal spelling, editing and formatting tests
- Highly proficient in Google Apps (Gmail for business, spreadsheets, docs, etc.) or equivalent MS Word, Outlook and Excel experience
- Excellent email and Internet research skills
- Excellent spelling and editing skills

Benefits:

- Quarterly bonus based on company performance (if we profit, so do you!)
- We promote and give raises based on skills learned; you can advance quickly.
- Office hours are Monday–Friday, 7:30am–4:30pm (schedule can vary around that), never on weekends
- We take all federal holidays off, paid (10–12 days!)
- We offer 2 weeks paid time off (PTO) to cover sick and vacation days in addition to federal holidays, which can be expanded as you grow with the company
- We have limited office hours between Christmas and New Years Eve
- No dress code: flip-flops and shorts are okay!
- Flex-time is available for this position (take an hour, make it up later, etc.)

MATT KNEE

- Open door policy (we listen to your issues/ideas), weekly meetings to address any employee issues
- Annual performance review
- Free coffee or soda of your choice
- Sorry, we do not provide health insurance at this time
- 401k plan with company matching up to 4%
- Advancement opportunities: we almost exclusively promote from within

There is an initial 30-day paid evaluation and training period after which we will determine if you are a good fit for our company. Small errors in our line of work can be expensive and time-consuming, so it is imperative that you are a detail-oriented person if you wish to apply for this job.

Here's how to apply:

1. Use the fields on this page to submit your application/resume.
2. Place my initials and a link to our company blog on the top your cover letter.
3. Your cover letter should be written below the initials and link. Tell us briefly why you would be a great fit for this job. Generic cover letters will probably be ignored due to the volume of resumes we typically receive.

We will be reviewing applications for the next week or so. If we determine that you are a match, we will call and email you for an interview. Due to the volume of resumes received, I may not be able to respond to each individually, but I will promise to go over each resume carefully.

Thanks, and I look forward to your application.
Sincerely,
Matt Knee
President and Founder
MyCompanyWorks, Inc.

STARTUPS MADE SIMPLE

I believe this ad has proven to work because of several factors:

1. We've described our company: who we are, what we do for our customers, how highly rated we are by the BBB, etc. I've even given the address so applicants can check how far it is from where they live (commute time is a big employee complaint).

2. We've clearly stated the exact qualifications (even including disqualifications), daily duties, and experience required.

3. We've clearly stated the pay and mentioned the bonus program.

4. We've listed the benefits of this job, and note that I'm even mentioning that we *don't* offer health insurance (which is a long story related to being small and multi-state, so I explain it carefully during phone interviews). Instead, I've made the pay higher than most Office Assistant jobs in my area to compensate for that and listed the many non-compensation benefits we offer.

5. I have what I call a "tripwire" at the end of the job ad that requires the applicant to have read down that far and pay attention to the requirements for submitting a resume. We use this for any job that requires a detail-oriented person (and most do).

This ad has been used, with few changes, for over a decade, and it has produced very good results (we modify it for other positions but mostly it's the same template). It's not perfect and doesn't always work (nothing *always* works when dealing with humans), but it's served us well over the years. You may not be able to offer some of the higher-end benefits like paid holidays or a 401k, but just do what you can to attract a higher caliber candidate and pay as well as you can afford.

MATT KNEE

Good Interviews and Assessments

A good job description and job ad should hopefully generate plenty of qualified applicants. Next, you'll want to learn some basic interview tactics and some kind of assessment or trial period so you can see if your candidate has the skills you need.

Identify your top ten or so candidates for each job, and then do a phone interview. A phone interview is a great way to filter out candidates and prevent the wasted time of too many in-person interviews. Set up phone interviews for these candidates and have a consistent way you talk to all of them (write out a script and checklist) so you can easily compare them to each other and also detect any potential issues, which we'll discuss below. Generally, you describe the job, ask specific questions of your candidates related to the job, clarify anything about their resume or availability, and ask them if they have questions. You can find many examples of questions and scripts online.

After phone interviews, you may wish to invite your top three or so candidates for an in-person interview. This is a good opportunity to show them around, let them get a feel for the company, and hear a detailed explanation of the job and what's expected. I often say that a good employee interview is more like "job dating;" you want to see it they're a good match for the job, your company, and even your personality and the personalities of your current team. This will give you a good opportunity to assess their interpersonal skills as well.

In-person interviews can be quick or long depending on how important the job is to your business. *Topgrading* and other books recommend very long, detailed interviews (several hours long), especially for higher-level positions. My philosophy on this is that it really depends on the job and skill-level for which you're hiring.

Lately, I have been leaning toward assessments and trial employment periods instead of very long interviews. Employee assessments are becoming very advanced and can even score employees based on how successful they are likely to be for the specific type of position you are offering (they have access to historical performance data from many other employees and companies). These can run from very simple 20-question tests to very long assessments for high-level executives. I have some listed in the Chapter Resources.

You can create your own assessments as well, but be careful about various employment laws when doing so. For example, if you are hiring for a detail-oriented clerical position, then create a spelling and editing test. If you're hiring for a chef, see how they prepare a specific dish.

Finally, more and more companies are simply hiring an employee as a contractor or for a trial period of a day, a week, or a month to see how they do the actual job. My company does 30-day trials for most new employees, and we assess how they're doing at the end of 30 days. If you've written the job description well and specified the expected results, it shouldn't be a hard decision to make after seeing the person do a job.

Hiring and interviewing is more of an art than a science, and improving your skills over time will add greatly to your business. I'm still learning things after 15+ years of hiring people. Remember to always verify what you do against your local laws. That said, here are some good practices for interviewing and assessing:

- **Clear dob descriptions and ads**. Again, you can't expect good results (or candidates) from vague job descriptions and ads. See the previous section.

- **Write good questions**. You'll want to come up with 3–5 questions directly related to the job you are filling ("How would you handle.." and "What is the best way to..." types of open-ended questions seem to work well) and ask the same questions of each candidate so you can compare them.

- **Threat of the reference check (TORC)**. *Topgrading* and other books recommend you do reference checks on all candidates. They even recommend you let candidates know you will be doing reference checks in the job ad and interviews and even have them arrange the call. The simple threat of a reference check will filter out a lot of bad candidates.

- **Watch for warning signs.** There are many of these you can find online, but some obvious warning signs during the interview (phone or in-person) include dishonesty, talking poorly about previous employers or supervisors, inability to recall work history, poor phone demeanor, poor interpersonal skills or sloppy appearance, etc. Many things depend on the job, so identify what's important to you and screen for that.

- **Use or create assessments.** As discussed, using a good assessment can help you really filter out bad candidates or at least see if they can do the actual job. Consider trial periods as well.

- **Screen for personality.** It's becoming more popular not to focus so much on credentials or experience but to instead focus on the type of personality that does well in a particular job. People with a great attitude and traits like helpfulness, conscientiousness, and a pleasant demeanor seem to do much better than others that are disagreeable and have a negative attitude. SWAN is also a well-known criteria which means: **S**marter than average, hard **W**orking, **A**mbitious, and **N**ice. Being thick-skinned (or not hyper-sensitive) is also a trait I've discussed that's valuable for startup employees.

- **Background check.** I background check all employees because we deal with credit cards and other sensitive information. I recommend that you background check any employee for anything remotely sensitive in your workplace. Some states have strict rules on this, so make sure to check.

- **Focus on accountability.** As I discuss in Superpower #14: Accountability Mindset, it's important for you to let each candidate know the results you expect and that they are accountable for these results. If you don't make it clear now, then it will be that much harder later.

Train and Onboard Properly

After you've chosen your candidate, send them a written job offer (and make sure to politely inform the candidates you took a pass on; you may need to call them back if this hire doesn't work out). Now, you'll want to bring this new hire onboard and train them.

This is where a lot of small businesses completely drop the ball by throwing a new employee to the wolves with zero resources or guidance. That's terrible for a lot of reasons but mostly because it starts everything off on the wrong foot, is awkward for the employee, and shows that you don't care that much how things operate (which also demonstrates low standards).

This doesn't have to be hard or complex. Make a simple list (save it and re-use it for other hires) of everything a new employee needs to do starting with a nice tour of everything (where to park, eat, bathrooms, etc.), meeting the team, doing hiring paperwork, setting up email or other accounts, learning about the company, etc., then going through their job description duties and learning how to do them properly.

Obviously, documented procedures here will help greatly, but at the least you'll want to train them personally or assign someone else to train them and be their "buddy" or mentor as they train. Show them exactly what "done" looks like and schedule regular follow-ups to check-in on their progress (or have their buddy keep you informed of progress).

People Management Best Practices

This topic also could be an entire book; it's not only important but probably the most difficult thing about owning a business. Managing employees, especially holding them accountable and having to confront the many problems and issues that dealing with humans entails, is not most people's favorite thing to do, especially entrepreneurs. In fact, poorly managing people or ignoring problems is how a lot of employee situations become bad in the first place.

The classic comedy movie *Office Space,* which details the dysfunctional management at the fictional company Initech, is one of my favorites and demonstrates the day-to-day frustrations of many modern office employees. It's actually pretty insightful about people management and the things we're discussing here.

Think about it, these guys just wanted some clear structure and communication (not eight different bosses and the same memo about TPS reports over and over) and some performance incentives (see the Leadership Superpower #15: Team Development and Motivation). Otherwise, why would Peter do more than the bare minimum?

Furthermore, they want the Right Tools (not a printer that was constantly broken), no silly dress code (see non-compensation benefits above), no empty platitudes about "Is this good for the company?" (try real Core Values or Principles instead), and to get rid of simple hassles around the office (the doorknob that shocks everyone and perhaps another office or location for the red-haired receptionist with the annoying phone voice).

I would even argue that they would probably have respected being held accountable for more than 15 minutes of real work a week, which would have given them a sense of accomplishment and maybe some pride in the job. Who knows, maybe Peter was just a bad hire in the first place (he did try to steal from the company after all) and could have been filtered out with decent interview skills. The point is that many of these seemingly small hassles build up and can make people crazy. However, problems can be fixed in a workplace, which doesn't have to be a corporate dystopia.

I think there are some pretty simple rules and best practices for managing a team:

- **Learn the leadership superpowers.** As I discussed in the chapter on leadership, there are many things to learn to master the management of employees, and it can be a struggle for many entrepreneurs and their managers. I highly recommend you review that chapter if necessary, especially with your managers (if you have any).

- **Hire, train and treat employees well.** It basically all comes down to that. The concept is not hard but the implementation can be challenging, and there are always employees who won't perform well no matter how well you do things.

- **Clearly defined job and expected results.** As we've discussed in this chapter quite a bit, the solution to a lot of employee issues is being absolutely clear on what is expected and the results they are supposed to achieve. If the job is clear and the definition of "done" is clear, then the performance should be clear against those measurements.

- **Measurable results.** Even better than clearly defined results are results you can measure. If you have measurable results that you've both agreed on, then when you are giving a review of an employee or need to coach them to better performance, you can point at a measurable number (like number of cold calls, number of orders processed, customer satisfaction %, etc.) and you will both know the truth with little space for argument over performance.

- **One person for one job.** I cringe when I see a "team" arrangement for some jobs (co-CEOs, co-managers or even two "leads" for a team of employees) because I can tell you right now: if two people are accountable for a job, then nobody is accountable and problems (the blame game) are not far behind. Make one person accountable for one job (starting with clear job descriptions). For example, if there are co-founders, make one the CTO (or COO, etc.) and the other the CEO. On a management team, make one person in charge of Operations and one in charge of Admin.

- **Staff properly.** Overworking a skeleton staff might be justified for a while in a startup, an emergency, or the loss of a key employee, but it shouldn't be standard practice. Make sure you staff adequately and make your team and managers accountable for letting you know when they need help or more people. Constant overtime or managers working in excess of 45 to 50 hours per week is a good indicator of this. Note that if managers are working that much but employees are not, then they likely have a delegation problem or are not being forthright about needing help.

- **Vision, purpose and goals.** As discussed earlier, having a clear vision and a purpose can be very motivating to founders and employees alike. It's always nice to know you're working toward something bigger than yourself. Goals are great to have because it feels great to meet or exceed them, especially if you reward your team for doing so.

- **Do meetings right.** Entire lifetimes could be wasted in ineffective and boring meetings. Employees mostly hate them. We'll go over this more in the Right Routines section later, but the key is to have meetings only if necessary, keep them focused on actionable solutions and decisions to be made, and keep them as short as possible.

- **Get things in writing.** If you're going to have a call, meeting, or face-to-face conversation about the business, make sure that the result is actionable with clear written decisions. Most employee, customer and founder disagreements can be avoided by clearly putting things in writing, even an email. Be wary of people who resist putting things in writing and demand it from your staff (it forces accountability).

- **Do regular reviews and 1-on-1s.** You should review each employee at least yearly (even more if you have the time) to review performance, adjust pay and/or promote or move to a better place for them (right person in the right seat). Many companies are adopting regular 1-on-1s (every month or two) between managers and their staff, and this seems to solve a lot of the problems and issues that we've discussed. It can be good to let an employee vent a bit and discuss their problems, goals and more. There are many resources online for effective 1-on-1s.

- **Good process.** As discussed in this chapter, having broken, undocumented, or no real process in your business is a recipe for chaos and employee frustration. Make having a good process part of your strategy for hiring, training and keeping good people.

- **Use an Issue List.** As described in the book *Traction* by Gino Wickman, an Issue List is a great way to de-hassle and solve problems within your company from both employees and customers (assuming you actually use it and fix the problems). We'll go over that more in the next section of this chapter on the Right Tools.

- **Praise and rewards.** Rewards, bonuses, and non-compensation benefits can definitely make life better for employees, but a simple "Hey, good job" and generous praise for a job well done is motivating to many employees. One caveat: Be wary of people who seem to need praise for just doing the bare minimum; this is often the sign of a poor-performing employee.

- **Delegate effectively.** If you don't learn how to delegate well, you'll simply say yes to every request from your team (or you'll just do it because you can do it faster and better) and work yourself to death. At the least, write procedures for the things you dislike doing and train others to do them. If you're overworked and don't delegate, then the company can never move forward, and you'll never earn your freedom. Delegation is also how you develop your team's skills.

- **Hand the monkey back.** Related to delegation, the book *The One Minute Manager and the Monkey* shows that a very effective tactic is to take your employees requests and "give the monkey back" to them so it's not on your back. For example, if an employee says that customers are having a hard time figuring out something about your product, you might tell them, "Will you please collect all the customers' names who are having this issue in a spreadsheet, send them an email asking for specific details on the problem, log the problems, and send me your ideas for fixing it by close of business Friday?" This builds problem-solving and accountability into your team and is a great way to help them take ownership of issues.

- **Honesty and trust.** Being honest, open, and willing to listen and debate ideas openly is a great way to build trust and accountability. Once you've built trust, then a lot of problems disappear because you know you can count on your team. If you're deceptive or break trust (or if they do), then bad things are going to happen.

- **How you work best.** Let others know how you work best, especially your managers and direct reports. For example, if you work late and prefer things via email (and that you don't expect replies to emails sent at 2:00 a.m. until business hours) or if you like anything done a certain way, then make sure to show them what that means exactly.

The rules are pretty straightforward; it's the actual living by these rules that's the hard part for almost every founder or manager I've ever encountered in business. People can be hard to deal with, and the better you get at it, the easier your life will be.

Managing Poor Performers and Toxic People

The final thing I want to go over on the topic of the Right People is what is generally considered the hardest part of people management: managing poor-performing or toxic employees. I think only a sociopath actually likes to tell people about their shortcomings or fire people but there are some best practices to doing this as well.

Let's start with what I call toxic people: Get rid of them. Toxic behavior includes constant complaining (without trying to solve the issue or even present it to those that can fix it), a negative attitude in general, pessimism, bullying or intimidating others (or customers), dishonesty, and my personal pet peeves: talking negatively about others behind their back and gossiping.

Listen, I like an honest, open and even aggressive discussion of ideas and problems, but that's not even close to what I'm talking about with toxic people. Toxic people make their teammates uncomfortable, angry or jealous (usually with incessant gossiping about others' salary, promotions, how they are performing, who they are dating, etc.) and generally drain the energy of everyone who has to deal with them.

I don't care if they're the best performer on your team; they still need to go. The one exception I'll make is if you somehow have some kind of super-genius with an incredibly rare talent working for you, then isolate that person (make them work from home) and minimize or eliminate their communication with your team. This is incredibly rare, so my default recommendation is to get rid of toxic people as soon as you can according to your employment laws. Make sure to document absolutely everything carefully because these are also the types that will "go legal."

People who are performing poorly, as long as they aren't toxic, are actually not very hard to deal with in comparison. The antidote to poor performance (and not hiring toxic people as well) are the many things we've mentioned in this chapter including clear job descriptions, expected or measurable results, hiring for good personality traits and having a good management system.

However, as any manager will tell you, even if you have all those things you're still going to have a few bad apples get through the process. Again, when dealing with humans this is to be expected, so don't let it ruin your day. Some simple coaching and a written plan to correct things is usually very effective.

The One Minute Manager and many other books show that a quick conversation that clarifies what's expected and corrects the behavior is a great start. If the issue happens again then you'll want to give a written warning specifying exactly what needs to change and by when (see examples of these online and in the book).

Finally, a "three strikes" rule is appropriate for most people: If you have to warn about the same issue three times then the person should be let go. If you do things right, this shouldn't even be a surprise to the employee and many of them will quit before the third strike because they know they may simply not be able to meet or even want to meet expectations.

A final word on doing warnings and firings is what I call "five minutes of pain." After you've clearly documented everything in writing and covered all the legal bases, just get the bad part over with as fast as possible. Don't torture yourself or your team with bad employees. Consider that maybe you might actually be freeing this person to move on to someplace better. Some people saying that getting fired was the best thing that ever happened to them because it forced them to change careers to something better or and removed them from an environment that wasn't ideal for them. Getting rid of toxic people and poor performers will dramatically improve your workplace so don't hesitate to take action.

The Right Tools

I joked about the *Office Space* printer earlier, but I'm actually dead serious. Things like that can be really annoying for your team. Whether they are actual tools like in a machine shop, the office machines you use every day or virtual tools like office supply lists, setting up the right tools in your company can be a great source of efficiency and effectiveness.

I've been to some companies that have a great product or service but when I peek in the office, there are old computers, a dot matrix printer, carbon copy invoices, a whiteboard for planning and scheduling, and they generally look like they're trapped a decade or two in the past. A company like this could definitely use some updated tools, especially if they're already providing a good product or service. Good tools will make them more effective and profitable.

Warning: A lot of people obsess on the tools only (for example, a fancy CRM system or productivity software) but I've learned the hard way (I've actually developed productivity software before based on this misguided assumption) that it's actually much more important for you to set up the other things well in your company, especially the Right Plan, the Right People and the Right Process before you focus too much on tools.

Sure, you can adopt the coolest new project management software in the world, but if you haven't figured out your vision, goals, leadership and how to execute and hold people accountable then the software is probably not going to meet your expectations and may actually be counterproductive. You'll likely be all over the place and only frustrate your team.

Once you've at least worked on those competencies in your business, The Right Tools for the job will be helpful because you've set up the underlying framework for a company that has a clear vision, has great goals, has great processes and hires great people and leads them effectively. You would ideally already have a system for getting things done well and adding great tools and systems will help you supercharge your effectiveness and can be a great competitive advantage.

Let's go over some great systems and tools you should consider for your company (I will recommend vendors for many of these in the Chapter Resources):

The Issue List

I've discussed The Issue List previously (from the book *Traction* by Gino Wickman) and the concept is very simple: if you, your employees or your customers have a problem, hassle or even an opportunity to improve or streamline something then add it to the list. Let any employee add to the list and make it available for everyone to see, mostly so they can see existing problems and how they're being prioritized and fixed.

Typically this will be a shared spreadsheet, task management software or even a simple whiteboard. Just make sure that it's easily available to everyone. Consider even setting up an issues@company.com email address to easily gather feedback from anyone.

Then, when you have your regular meetings (see the Right Routines), one part of that will be prioritizing, discussing and solving these issues one by one. You might consider having a private list for sensitive or employee issues. This sounds simple but it's incredibly effective. Imagine all the various problems, hassles and frustrations in your company being solved one by one. This is how you build a great company and it will show your team you care about their problems as well.

The only rules I really have for the Issue List are 1) if an employee adds an issue, they need to add what their proposed solution to the problem is, which puts them in problem-solving mode rather than complaining mode and 2) if something is very urgent then feel free to email first with all the details and then determine if it can wait until the next meeting to discuss. If so, "hand the monkey back" and ask them to post it to the Issue List.

Team Calendar

This should be pretty obvious but I think it's valuable to have a "top level" view of the company and the many tasks or events that need to be done at or by a specific time. A good digital calendar that everyone can access is a valuable tool to have because it is a central place to see what the future looks like and gets everyone on the same page.

Add things like recurring meetings, recurring tasks (weekly, monthly, etc.), scheduled time off for key employees, employee birthdays, federal holidays, and even reminders of things like sending out holiday cards to customers or doing a seasonal sale or promotion. A good calendar is key to organizing your systems.

Task or Project Management System

Depending on the type of work your company does, you may need anything from simple checklists to very advanced project management software to make sure people get things done. I went over this pretty thoroughly in the Personal Productivity Superpower but my only real standing rule for task or project management software is that it's available on all your devices and that it has recurring tasks (so you can begin setting up and delegating recurring procedures).

One more thing I'll add is that it's probably better to get your team all on the same system now rather than a hodge-podge of paper and various software solutions. Accountability will be easier if you can see all the tasks assigned to people and the status of those tasks or projects. A good software system will allow you to manage your personal to-do's privately so if you can get everything in one system that will dramatically simplify your life.

Shared Drive

These days there are several very reliable data storage drives that can be accessed from any device. This is a huge time saver, especially for companies that utilize a lot of documents. The most important thing is that it is organized well and that proper security (consider encryption) and permissions are installed for sensitive documents. A good start to your drive structure would be something like this:

- Private Files (your own private files not accessible to others)
- Shared Company Files (then broken down by folder: Communications, Documents, Procedures, etc.)
- Shared Customer Files (store all customer files or create folders for big projects or clients)
- Archives (storage is so cheap that it's easier to just save all old or outdated files in this folder for safekeeping).

Intranet

It's been said that an average office employee spends 20% of their day just looking for information and documents. A central website securely accessible to all employees by any device can be an incredible time saver and productivity booster. In my business, our intranet, which we call "Central" is where we:

- Post notices and birthday wishes to employees (keeping them out of email)
- Link to The Issue List, Team Calendar, Training and Onboarding tools
- Store our written procedures and instructions for updating and writing new ones
- Keep information about our products and services
- Store handbooks, time off requests and other documents
- Maintain contacts, phone and account numbers for vendors and other important contacts
- Document our more complex systems like servers and our custom-built CRM system
- Keep tracking documents like inventory and office supply lists (one for each location)

The Scoreboard

How can everyone on your team quickly see how the company (and teams/individuals) is doing right now versus the goals you've set? As mentioned, having an easy to see Scoreboard for everyone to look at is not only very clarifying but can be motivational — like watching your team win or advance toward a shared goal. Some companies put this on a whiteboard, on their intranet, send it out weekly via email or even stream it to a TV where everyone in the office can see it.

The Manual

Any well-run franchise has an "operations manual" that tells the franchise owner how to run every aspect of their business from opening the office/store, to managing employees and providing their product or service. In Step 6 we'll go over putting The Manual together but it's important to start documenting your procedures and centralizing your various management checklists and systems as described in the beginning of this chapter. Ideally The Manual would be accessible from your intranet.

Communication Systems

Your communication systems will include your phone system, employee cell phones, email, chat and other systems. The particular setup will vary dramatically based on your needs so the main advice I can give is to put some thought and planning into your communication systems because while constant communication might *seem* like a great idea, it can actually be very disruptive and prevent your team from getting any Real Work done. Also, do you really want to be available and reachable by everyone at all hours of the day? That might seem ideal at first but it gets old quickly, trust me. At the least I recommend that if you're not technically inclined (and probably even if you are) that you utilize a cloud provider for most of your communications simply because they will be supported and consistently updated.

Customer Relationship Management (CRM) or Help Desk Software

It's been joked that one way to run a successful private equity firm (firms that buy, improve, then sell other companies for a big profit) is to find a company with several million dollars in sales but without a help desk or CRM system, then buy the company and simply install and train on the software to dramatically increase the company's value.

Seriously though, a CRM or help desk can drastically improve how you sell or service your clients. It's very powerful to centralize all the customer data in one place (accessible to all employees), have access to their entire history, keep detailed notes and have things like email templates, due dates and even performance reporting.

Like everything else, the key is pick the right system and implementing it well. Once you've done that, put one person in charge of service or sales and create measurable goals for things like response time, customer ratings and more.

Process Management Software

As I mentioned in The Right Process, there are now many great solutions for tracking and documenting recurring processes, procedures and tasks. We use these at my company and they're a game changer if implemented correctly. Imagine having a dashboard where you could see and track the status of every workflow or procedure in your business.

You can create "activated" checklists and workflows (meaning you track when each step is completed, and by whom, instead of someone doing them in their head) for each of your processes or procedures (for example, an Onboarding Checklist). Each checklist is assigned, has an accountable person and is accessible from all devices. For a process oriented company, this is life in the next realm and a huge source of freedom.

Website

It should be obvious but I believe every business should have a website, even a simple one page site. It's important to realize that younger generations have no concept of the "yellow pages" and that the vast majority of research on business is done online now. Seriously, if you don't have a website you may as well not exist to a large percentage of the population. I recommend at the least that you secure your domain name, use one of the many "site builder" services to get your basic website up as soon as possible and then continue to add information, FAQs, content and even blog regularly to show people that you are actively in business.

Custom Built Systems

I'll briefly mention custom software systems, mostly because we use them heavily and there are some important things to keep in mind about them (especially if you are building a system as your product). First, a huge percentage of big software projects are late, over budget or simply outright fail. I've seen a small business waste six figures on a failed project. Second, custom software is so difficult that you should always try to find existing software to manage your business if you can or a systems integrator who can customize existing software (instead of building it from scratch).

Writing extremely clear software specifications, providing screenshots, mockups of what the final product should look like and written narratives on exactly how a custom system needs to work is absolutely critical. Do in-depth research on writing great specifications, hiring great developers and managing a project including penalties to the firm or developers for missing deadlines. Carefully review legal contracts with them and be wary of foreign contractors who have little incentive to abide by US law. Trust me on this, entire years can be lost to technical projects gone bad. Finally, consider hiring a few different developers or firms for a small test project to see how effectively they work then working with the best one.

Tool Mastery

The last thing I'll say about Tools is that there is a remarkable difference between people that have mastered their tools and those that have not. What I mean is that almost every tool can be customized or tweaked to work best for an individual or team.

I see a lot of people never even bother to check the settings or research the best practices, tips and tricks for their task manager, chat, calendar, email, etc. and they aren't optimizing how the tool should work for them. For example, too many notifications is a problem I see a lot and many people won't take two minutes to find adjust the settings. This is a huge waste because many of these tools are not effective "out of the box" and need to be adapted to your workflow and style.

The Right Routines

They key to putting this all together is establishing consistent routines to make sure everyone is clear on The Plan, continually optimizing The Process, The People are getting things done (according to The Plan) and making sure everyone has The Right Tools. This mainly consists of a few well-run meetings and a lot of great communication (review Superpower #13: Good Communication Skills).

The Meetings

Depending on the size of the company, you'll want to have regular meetings to keep everyone aligned and solve problems.

If you're a small team, all working in the same room, this may not be necessary too often but as your team gets larger or are in several locations you'll want to schedule regular meetings (eventually you'll have separate management and departments meetings). The point is to make sure you have a clear agenda and time limit for each meeting otherwise they'll go off topic and people will start dreading them.

Team Meeting:

Do this meeting the same day and time each week (or less) and set a hard time limit, an hour is usually plenty of time. Here's a good agenda framework:

- **The Plan.** Make sure everyone is crystal clear on all aspects of The Plan. Discuss any proposed updates.

- **The progress and numbers.** How you are doing according to The Plan, your goals and a review of the Scoreboard. What needs to be done to improve or get them on track?

- **The Issue List.** You will agree on the top issues to work on, discuss, brainstorm and solve them one by one until time runs out. I recommend you set a timer to go off 5 minutes before the end of the scheduled meeting so you can wrap it up with the next steps.

- **Accountability.** At the end of the meeting, you (or your managers) will assign any tasks to each team member, when that task is due and if they have any questions about the task and then agree on the due date. Put this in writing or your task management system.

- **Send a summary.** To get the whole company aligned, consider sending out a short email that lists The Plan, The Scoreboard, any Issues you've solved and the tasks that were assigned. Remember that repetition is important for aligning teams.

- **Quarterly planning.** Quarterly and yearly you'll want to meet to review your strategy, review and set goals in separate meetings specifically on these topics.

Daily Huddle

As mentioned in the Communication Skills Superpower, a great way to start the day is with a Daily Huddle. The purpose of this is to start the day out on a good note, give your team an update and mention anything that is blocking you from doing your job at the moment (questions, concerns you may have, limited to one minute per person). What this does is cut down on interruptions throughout the day and makes sure the team is aligned and knows what it needs to get done today. Check online for best practices and videos of great Daily Huddles.

Employee Reviews and 1-on-1s

Regular employee reviews should be calendared and done at least yearly. Many managers have started doing regular 1-on-1s (as mentioned previously) to get and give feedback on performance so there are no "surprises" at the annual review. It's also a great time to get to know the employee and what their future plans and desires are with the company.

That's pretty much it for routines. Have your regular Team Meeting, your Daily Huddle and Reviews. The key is making sure you actually do them. Routines are how you will solve problems and continually improve this management system you have built.

Summary

We've covered a *lot* of ground in this chapter (many books take hundreds of pages to cover these topics) so don't think that you need to implement it all today. As mentioned in the beginning, focus on The Plan, The Process or The People (start with whichever is your biggest challenge) and set aside regular time to actively build and optimize your management system with consistent Routines which will ultimately be the key to your freedom as a business owner.

Visit http://www.startupsmadesimple.com for Chapter 9 Resources and to download the Startups Made Simple Strategic Plan and Example Written Procedure.

10
STEP SIX: SYSTEMIZE IT

"Whenever you see a successful business, someone once made a courageous decision." —Peter F. Drucker

The first step in systemizing a business is to have a systems mindset. So many founders and employees get this wrong that I would consider it an epidemic in small business. You want to think of your business as a complete system. Continue to integrate, automate, orchestrate, simplify and unify your systems, marketing and branding into one unified whole. Systemizing and documenting things over time compounds like interest and you continue to add value to your business.

It may take a while and some practice to get your management system working nicely. It'll always be a work in progress so don't demand perfection. Once you think you've mastered The Five Competencies we discussed in the previous chapter (and are of course making enough money) you can start thinking about taking this machine you've built to the next and final level — a beautiful and systemized business.

Orchestration

Orchestration is a fancy word for making sure all the disparate parts of your business are working well together. Think of an orchestra and how many different instruments (tools) work together to produce a beautiful piece of music. That's what we want for our systemized business: many parts working beautifully together in a machine that is well-run, well-organized and could be operated by pretty much anyone with a reasonable amount of training and guidance.

The E-Myth by Michael Gerber describes this with a great story about a beautifully run small hotel in California. The entire experience from checking in (where they casually ask what type of coffee and newspaper you prefer), how clean the rooms are (which is then stocked with your favorite coffee and newspaper), the wonderfully maintained grounds where the lights come on perfectly at sunset and how every experience seems to have been not only well thought-out, but perfected for the peak guest experience.

Gerber then goes on to describe how he meets the manager of the hotel and how relaxed he seems to be; this is not a stressed out person scurrying from problem to problem putting out fires. When asked how he manages all of this perfection and is so relaxed, he simply pulls out the color-coded operations manual and basically says "It's all in here." Whether he's the founder or a manager hired by the founder/owner is not really relevant; the key is that the business is systemized and organized so well that everything is in one place and can be easily managed from one manual.

This is the level of orchestration and organization that I visualize for a systemized business. The key is getting The Five Competencies from the previous chapter down first, but then developing what I call "The Manual" for your business.

The Manual

Imagine having one manual, either physical or virtual (or both) that you could easily reference to guide you through the various complexities of your business. It would centralize everything you know about running your business and even include the history of the business and its written procedures so others could be taught to run things. That's the vision of The Manual. It includes the history and purpose of the business, training materials, written procedures, checklists for routines and is the key to a systemized business.

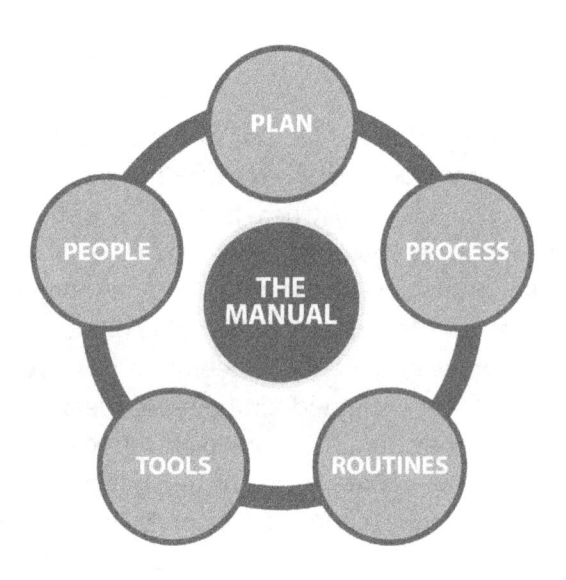

If you owned a business like this, you could run it yourself or hire others to run it for you — it's up to you and what you like to do. Maybe you'll decide that you want to run it yourself for a few years then hire someone else to grow and manage it. Perhaps you want to sell the business at some point. The point is any stress about the future of the company will be massively reduced allowing you to focus on the here and now. The Manual makes all of these things not only possible but much easier and adds considerable monetary value to your business.

Now imagine a business that does not have anything like The Manual. Maybe some things are written down but most are not, they mostly live in either the owner's head or the heads of their employees. Employees are constantly asking the owner how to do things or solve problems because nothing is documented (meaning the owner can never step away or take a real vacation). If the employee who knows how to do some things quits or the owner gets sick (or worse) the business is screwed, at least temporarily. Their stress level, like that of most small business owners, is probably pretty high with various "what if" nightmare scenarios that they're not prepared to handle.

When it comes time to move on and think about selling or retiring, or burnout sets in (which is common among business owners with poorly managed businesses), the business is not really worth much because it's not a system that can be easily purchased and learned (like a franchise). It's totally owner or employee dependent so it won't be worth much to a potential buyer and if you want to hire someone to take it over they'll need constant hand-holding for months because nothing is documented.

With that cautionary tale out of the way, let's focus on how to get our manual started and what we should include in it.

- **About the Company.** Write the founding story and a clear narrative about your product/service. For training purposes, it's extremely valuable to write a few pages on how and why your company was founded and also give a great overview of the products and services your company offers. This is great for new employees to get a grasp of the company history and what your company does for your customers. It will give them a good introduction to the rest of the manual.

- **Organizational Chart**. Have an organizational chart organized by function (not by person — for example "Operations Manager" not "Dave") so everyone is clear on the structure of the company and how decisions are made. This also clarifies who reports to who and where people may want to work in the future.

- **The Plan.** As discussed in The Right Plan in Step 5, getting everyone on the same page and making sure they understand the purpose, vision and goals of the company is incredibly valuable.

- **The Core Values or Principles.** We'll discuss these later in the chapter, but once your company is established you'll want to set a handful of Core Values or Principles to further streamline decision-making and clarify behavior in your company.

- **Job Descriptions.** Step 5 went over job descriptions and how important they are. Keep these in your manual and keep them updated as jobs change over time. Now everyone can see not only what's expected of them but of the other people in the company (or other jobs they may want to do).

- **Routines.** In the Right Routines we discussed about keeping regular meetings to keep your whole system optimized and on plan. Mention your meetings and any major recurring procedures (for example, monthly closing of books, etc.) you think are important to be documented.

- **Written Procedures.** As discussed in The Right Process in Step 5, get your big processes and procedures written down (especially the complex ones). Once you have most of your procedures written, life becomes much easier and your manual becomes much more valuable. Include instructions for writing new and updating existing procedures.

- **Tools.** List your major systems and tools (like we did in The Right Tools) and either provide direct instructions on how to use and maintain them or at least link or mention where the "help" materials and manuals can be located.

- **Branding or Style Guide.** A big part of systemizing is unifying the look, feel and even the personality of your company and making sure it's consistent across everything you do. This can be as simple as picking your company colors, logo, font and tagline then making sure it's documented and known by all. One way I can usually detect a well-systemized company is if their website, emails, colors, logo and even the style of communication and their advertisements are all remarkably consistent.

- **Policies.** Either list your policies or link or reference separate employee manuals and other policies (security policies, etc).
- **Version and Last Updated.** Give each version of The Manual a version number like 1.4, 1.5, etc. and put it right on the cover so everyone can know they have the most recent one. Also indicate the date it was last updated so you can make sure that version includes any recent changes.

The Manual will change your life for the better and is the key to your freedom. However, like everything in life, there are some issues to address if you want to thrive well into the future, even with a beautifully systemized business.

- **System Complexity and Entropy**
- **Core Values or Principles**
- **Building a Leadership Team**
- **Planning for the Future**

System Complexity and Entropy

"Fools ignore complexity. Geniuses remove it."
—Alan Perils

After you've built The Manual and have The Five Competencies under control, it's important to beware of things that will slowly erode your system: complexity and entropy. In simple terms, stuff will start to get more complex as you grow and The Manual may soon be outdated and systems may start to break down.

You're probably thinking: *Damn, I just got things in order and now he's telling me it will all fall apart.* No, as in other parts of the book, I'm just giving you some things to watch out for and prevent before they even happen. A lot of books go into the building of the system but not necessarily the scaling and maintenance of the system.

The main thing to keep in mind is the Systems Mindset, how all the various pieces of your business work together now and how even small changes can cause unforeseen problems. If you recall the Five Competencies — The Right Plan, The Right Process, The Right People, The Right Tools, The Right Routines — you can see that they're all pretty interrelated and dependent on each other. It starts with The Plan, and changes to that may affect Process, People, Tools and Routines. A change to the Tools might interfere with Process. Process changes can affect everything and so on. The point is a change in one area likely requires a change in the others.

The vast majority of founders and employees don't understand how "one little change" or tweak to a system can cause chaos or complexity in unforeseen ways. For example, say someone changes a minor procedure to require a certain approval (perhaps with good intentions, to prevent some kind of error or problem encountered previously) going forward. Great idea — or so we all think!

What may not be obvious are the second-order-effects (see the Good Decisions Superpower for more on that) of that tiny change. Let's say that the supervisor "Dave" is in charge of these new approvals and soon he's spending 25% of his day reviewing and approving what is actually a pretty minor procedure and not mission critical. Soon Dave is overwhelmed (and the way work gets done has a huge bottleneck, even worse when Dave is on vacation), falls behind on his other work, gets frustrated or has to hire additional help to manage it all.

So, not only have we added complexity to the procedure, we've added additional work and even employees to manage it. Perhaps it was important enough to warrant it but the point is that making little changes can have big effects so it's important to think them through and not just implement them without much thought.

Perhaps we could have eliminated or automated the approval process. The same principle applies to the other systems. If you change your strategy, products, services, etc. these will all have ripple effects and cascade throughout the business. On a related note, if you allow one employee to do things differently or live by a different set of rules, you're going to have problems.

So how do we prevent this? Here are a few ways:

- Explain System Complexity and Entropy in The Manual and as a part of training. Being aware of the problem is a big way to prevent it.

- As the accountable person, Dave should communicate the issue to those who can change it immediately. This is the power of building an accountable organization; people will notice issues and bring them to those that can solve them.

- For every new rule, process or procedure you add, try to eliminate or streamline another. As I mentioned in The Right Process, a quarterly review of a major process for ways to streamline and optimize is a great idea.

- Always be simplifying: product, procedures, training, etc. The key is to make the internal operations of your business so efficient and simple that nobody will be able to compete with your efficiencies, which gives you advantages in speed, service and cost.

- Keep a balance between innovation and compliance. You don't want to get in any legal or tax trouble as described in the previous chapter but you also don't want to become so compliance and rule obsessed that your company cannot innovate or is completely hogtied by HR or compliance issues that nothing ever gets done.

- Core Values or Principles can help guide intelligent decisions. For example, if your Core Value is "Simplicity" then it should be obvious that adding complexity to a procedure should be, at the least, closely scrutinized. More on that in the next section.

Keeping our Systems Mindset, we also need to be careful about what Verne Harnish describes in his book *Scaling Up* as "the valley of death." To quickly summarize, companies tend to reach levels of growth and then stagnate or even fall off, typically at $1 million (only 4% make it), $10 million (only 1% make it), $50 million, etc. in annual revenue.

A company may reach $1 million quickly then will struggle to get to the next level because the systems and people that got them to $1 million are usually very different than what they need to get to the next level and this process continues as the company grows more complex.

A good way to prevent this is to make sure your various systems adapt and grow with the company. The Leadership Superpowers are also good to review. Next, we'll go into some other ways to get your company to the next level: Core Values and building a Leadership Team.

Core Values or Principles

> *"Simple, clear purpose and principles give rise to complex and intelligent behavior. Complex rules and regulations give rise to simple and stupid behavior."* —Dee Hock

The purpose of Core Values or Principles is to simplify decision-making with a small handful of easily remembered, constantly reinforced reminders of your values or principles. Remember that in the Good Communication Superpower we discussed how complexity explodes by 400% when you add even one more person to a small team? Imagine that with 10, 50 or 100+ people. Things get so complex they fall apart or the organization gets hopelessly inefficient trying to manage it all.

A handful of Core Values or Principles can streamline decision-making and encourage good behavior throughout the business to the lowest levels so communication is not so complex. Well-discovered Core Values or Principles also make the future direction and strategy of the business more clear. They make delegating easier because they can guide the person whom you've trusted to do your work.

So how do we discover them? There are a lot of tools and exercises online that you can research but an easy way to take a first swipe is to simply list the traits you admire about the team you have (and good team members from the past), combine them into related concepts and "take them for a spin" for a few months to see if they feel right. I've listed some examples in the Chapter Resources. Some other best practices include:

- Avoid the obvious platitudes like "honesty", "integrity", "teamwork". First of all, these are unoriginal so your team won't feel they are genuine. Second, all employees should have these values by default. There's no special reward for being "honest" for example; everyone should be honest or they shouldn't be working at your company in the first place.

- Try to keep it to a memorable number of principles or values. Five is a good starting point. Amazon has 14 Principles and Zappos has 10 but the general consensus is that the shorter the list, the easier it is to remember.

- Consider Operating Principles as described by Sam Carpenter in his book *Work the System*. For a more process-oriented business, a list of Operating Principles can clarify the many procedural working parts of a business into a clear simple list.

Build a Leadership Team

Freedom for you may be as simple as hiring a good manager or managers to take over day-to-day management of your small business. If that's your definition of your dream business then that's a great place to be once you systemize things. If your ambitions are larger than that, then truly taking your company to the next level will require building a proper Leadership Team.

I would say the main difference between a Management Team and a Leadership Team is that managers will keep your business running well and maybe even growing but probably still need your guidance and expertise. A proper Leadership Team will strategize and lead the company to much higher levels of revenue and performance, even without your direction. You may not even be the smartest person in the room (and probably shouldn't be) if you've hired the right Leadership Team. These people will be smart, clear-thinking, execution-obsessed and may even leave you in the dust provided you can find and recruit them (they can be hard to find.)

Needless to say, this is an advanced topic and probably the last "great hurdle" to going from a small business to one of the elite few businesses that get to $10 million sales and beyond. Here's what I've learned on this topic so far (and continue to learn):

- **The Leadership Superpowers**. As thoroughly discussed, these can be helpful to you not only to help you become more effective, but to see exactly what and who you need to take the company to the next level. This is often *not* the founder who is usually the bottleneck, as discussed. Especially consider the Communication Superpower and how you design your incentives.

- **Get out of the way**. Speaking of bottlenecks, the company is never going to get anywhere if you don't start delegating and start getting out of your own way. Yes, I know, only you can do certain things the "right way" and it's easier if you just do them. (Note: I'm rolling my eyes at this.) That mindset will get you nowhere fast. Only do the things you enjoy and delegate the rest. In our Organizational Chart mentioned earlier, begin by replacing yourself on that chart one by one.

- **Be a bit reckless**. I know, this sounds counter to almost everything I've said in this book but bear with me. To get to the next level, you may have to take some bigger risks, make some expensive hires (great hires should easily pay for themselves many times over if done right) and even tolerate a bit of chaos as your systems and people deal with everything. As I mentioned before, a good "managed chaos" can be tolerable and even necessary for a while.

- **Maintain The Five Competencies**. Your strategy will become more and more important as you grow so make sure to keep your plan updated and refer to it endlessly. Make sure everyone is on the same page, especially as you keep adding more staff. Keep Processes, People, Tools and Routines updated as well as you can as things change.

- **Focus on learning and training**. Leadership teams and employees of companies become more important as you scale. You'll actually begin to focus much more on developing your employees and spend more resources on training them as business gets more competitive.

- **Get great at goal setting and execution**. As you get more experience, you'll get much better at setting goals that are the "sweet spot" of aggressive but attainable. Great goal setting, especially in pursuit of a BHAG (as discussed in Superpower #6: Clear Goals) teamed with the execution Superpowers is incredibly powerful and a key to getting to the next level.

- **Do Real Work**. As I mentioned in the Productivity Superpower, there's a difference between Real Work and Process Work. Real Work is what moves your company forward and accomplishes goals. Process Work is what you need to get done every day to serve your customers but doesn't really improve anything. Doing Process Work all day will never move your company forward. Know the difference and realize that your employees will likely confuse the two.

There can obviously be a lot more to this topic and I highly recommend some books and even personal coaching if you want to build out a Leadership Team. A good coach who has been there before and can guide you is easily worth the expense.

Preparing for The Future

As we near the end of this book, there are a few more things that can be discussed to help ensure the survival and success of this systemized dream business we're building. It's human nature to get comfortable, especially if you have a successful thriving business, so I want to briefly cover them so that you're aware of and can prepare for them.

It's so cliche to say, but business really is moving faster than ever and doesn't seem likely it will slow down. While I think you should enjoy your systemized business and take plenty of long, relaxing vacations, if you intend to keep the business and want it to thrive then yes, I recommend you do some basic planning for the future and will give you my final list. This includes:

- **Future strategy.** Now that you have a nicely systemized business that's running great, it's time to step away and focus on the big picture items. This is a lot easier now that you have time to think so start thinking big about how you want this company to evolve and survive in the fast-paced business world. Spend time regularly thinking how to expand and improve your business. Use the skills from Step 1 to continue to imagine great things for your business. Think about how you would even destroy your business if you were a competitor so you can think of vulnerabilities you may want to address. A regular SWOT (Strengths, Weaknesses, Opportunities and Threats) analysis is a good idea. Think of your profit as letting you have time to figure out big things and run experiments.

- **Beware the Innovator's Dilemma.** This book by Clayton M. Christensen details how the things that your business has done to be successful over the years may actually be the seeds of your undoing and decline into lower sales and irrelevance. Don't start panicking about this right away but pick up the book or research the concepts online and start to think strategically about your business and how to prevent this from happening in your business.

- **Financial planning.** If you've got a great business, it would be foolish not to speak to a financial advisor and attorney about protecting this valuable asset. Think of a full legal review for any vulnerabilities and consider setting up a trust or other financial instruments to protect this asset (especially from predatory lawyers and consumers) and consider a succession plan for the future owner of your company.

- **Prepare for sale.** If you eventually want to sell your business, besides already having a well-systemized business there are some best practices you can do as you get close to putting it up for sale that can dramatically increase the value. There's a wealth of information online but it basically includes many of the things we've covered and why having a system you can sell is much more valuable than a regular business.

- **Continue to add value.** As your business becomes more streamlined and integrated, make sure you are building your brand, registering trademarks, copyrights, patents, business methods and more to further add value to your business.

- **Do the math: Sell or hire a CEO?** Here's a secret: A lot of people who sell their small or medium size business only get a few years of living expenses from the sale (sometimes from businesses they've run for decades) and the process of selling is long and time-intensive. Systemizing is one great way of increasing the value of your business beyond that but have you considered just hiring a manager or CEO and keeping the company going indefinitely? Think about it: For a few hours per month you could probably maintain the company with even a moderately competent CEO and still earn profits for many years to come. Something to think about.

We've covered a lot of ground in this book. I'm appreciative of anyone who stuck with me throughout and am extremely proud of anyone who puts in the work to imagine, start, grow, manage and systemize their dream business. As I mentioned in the introduction you're making the world a better place through your business. In the final part of this book I have two simple scorecards you can use to get a sense of your Superpowers and your business in general, followed by a brief conclusion.

Onward!

**Visit http://www.startupsmadesimple.com
for Chapter 10 Resources.**

PART THREE
The Scorecards

There are two simple scorecards in this section:

1. **The Founder Superpowers Scorecard** which helps you determine how well you are doing on acquiring the superpowers (or hiring others to take that function).

2. **The 6-Step Scorecard** which goes through the main points of each step and allows you to quickly determine how you're currently implementing your vision.

Tip: Complete a scorecard every few months to see how you're doing (and for your team as well if you'd like).

**Visit http://www.startupsmadesimple.com
to download digital versions of these scorecards
and tools that are mentioned.**

THE FOUNDER SUPERPOWERS SCORECARD

The Founder Superpowers	Score (1-5)
Energy	
Superpower #1: Health	
Superpower #2: Perseverance	
Superpower #3: Optimism	
Superpower #4: Momentum	
Vision	
Superpower #5: Clear Vision	
Superpower #6: Clear Goals	
Superpower #7: Product Obsession	
Execution	
Superpower #8: Agency Mindset	
Superpower #9: Resourcefulness	
Superpower #10: Personal Productivity	
Superpower #11: Good Decisions	
Superpower #12: Problem Solving	
Leadership	
Superpower #13: Good Communication Skills	
Superpower #14: Accountability Mindset	
Superpower #15: Team Development and Motivation	
Superpower #16: Courage to be Disliked	

THE 6-STEP SCORECARD

The Founder Superpowers

- ❏ I've completed the Founder Superpowers Scorecard and know where I currently stand.

- ❏ I've identified my best superpower category (e.g. "Execution") and I know to continue to develop this superpower.

- ❏ I've identified my worst superpower category so I know either to work on it or hire others to handle this superpower.

Step 1: Imagine It

- ❏ I've identified my primary motivation for starting a business and am committed to making it a burning desire.

- ❏ I have a Clear Vision (written) for the perfect business for me.

- ❏ My business idea is the best possible cross-section of what I like to do, what I'm good at, what's needed and what I can be paid for (ikigai).

- ❏ I've written my idea down in the Startups Made Simple Business Idea Generator (BIG) to clarify my thinking and prepare for the planning step.

Step 2: Plan It

- ❏ I understand it's important to test my idea so I can avoid wasting resources and time on a business idea that won't work.

- ❏ I'm aware of "professional bummers" and others who don't seem to like any new ideas and will avoid sharing my ideas with them for this reason.

- ❑ I'm aware of the top reasons for business failure and have crafted my business plan to avoid them.
- ❑ I've reviewed the best practices for picking a business name and have chosen a name for this project.
- ❑ I've completed the Startups Made Simple Business Plan to test my idea and do some "back of the napkin" math to see if I should proceed to the next step or go back to Step 1.
- ❑ I've tested my idea with some potential customers and at least 5 have indicated they would pay me immediately if my product or service existed.

Step 3: Start It

- ❑ I've determined if I need a formal business plan to obtain funding or investors.
- ❑ I've clarified ownership issues mentioned in Step 3 including agreeing on ownership percentage, duties and time commitments in writing (and stock options if applicable).
- ❑ I've selected a state, a name and legal structure appropriate for my business.
- ❑ I've filed the legal paperwork to formally register my business.
- ❑ I've completed the Startups Made Simple Startup Checklist to complete any post-formation tasks (bank accounts, licenses, etc.) to complete the proper set up of my business.

Step 4: Grow It

- ❑ I know the difference between sales and marketing and that they are both critical skills to learn for a startup to succeed.

- ❑ I understand that it is much easier to identify your ideal customer and target them (even in a small niche) then attempt to get your message out to every potential customer.
- ❑ I'm aware of the biggest marketing and sales mistakes (see Step 4) and have taken action to prevent them in my business.
- ❑ I understand that a superior product or service is easier to sell (but doesn't necessarily sell itself).
- ❑ I understand that some customers are much more profitable than others and I think "80/20" when trying to identify them.
- ❑ I've completed the Startups Made Simple Marketing Plan to identify my ideal customer, their personas, to build my list and test my message via various marketing methods.
- ❑ I'm aware of the elements of a great sales process, what makes great salespeople and have taken action to create a replicable sales process in my business.
- ❑ I'm aware of what it costs me to acquire a lead or sale and the lifetime value of a customer so I can adjust my marketing resources accordingly.
- ❑ I realize that I may need to pivot my idea to find "product market fit" and that this is normal in a startup. If I've exhausted the options I know it's normal to return to Steps 1 and 2 to continue working on my idea.

Step 5: Manage It

- ❑ I understand that having a management system for my business is key to earning my freedom from working *in* the business and to start working on improving the business.
- ❑ I'm aware of the Five Competencies:

- ❏ The Right Plan — I need to have a clear vision, purpose and goals.
- ❏ The Right Process — I need to have my processes documented.
- ❏ The Right People — I need to hire, train and manage the best people I can afford.
- ❏ The Right Tools — I need the best tools to do the job.
- ❏ The Right Routines — I need a regular routine to keep my business on track.
- ❏ I have scheduled regular time to work on the Five Competencies in my business (usually starting with Plan, Process or People) and implement the best practices as described in Step 5.
- ❏ I'm aware of the customer, money and compliance best practices as described in Step 5 and have taken action to prevent any issues in these areas.

Step 6: Systemize It

- ❏ I understand the importance of having a systems mindset and how it not only makes my life easier, but adds considerable value to my business.
- ❏ I've begun putting together "The Manual" and documenting my business as described in Step 6.
- ❏ I'm aware of how complexity and entropy can destroy my system so I've taken measures to prevent that in my business.
- ❏ I've adopted Core Values or Principles and use them regularly in my business.
- ❏ I've decided what I want for the future of this company and have planned accordingly (keep running it, hire a leadership team, hire a CEO, exit plan, etc.).

CONCLUSION

I end this journey with you, firmly in the latter parts of Step 6 myself. My business is systemized and I'm in the process of taking it to the next level. It took me 17 long years to get here — some of that time was very difficult and I would even call excruciating. That's the reason I wrote this book: to make sure others can get this done *much* faster and *much* easier. I hope that I've accomplished that goal.

Building a business is hard. It will likely change your mindset about many things — permanently. You'll look at the world differently after being responsible for a business, making payroll and more. The best part is that regardless if you fail or succeed, you've tried what most people won't and will likely have experienced things and learned skills that will serve you forever.

In the introduction, I mentioned the high failure rate of businesses. If you've reached this point in the book and managed to beat the odds (or are in the process of beating the odds) and are building and systemizing your dream business, you are truly living in the next realm my friend. I heartily congratulate you and would love to hear your success story (or any improvements or feedback to this book) and buy you a drink if you're ever in Las Vegas. My email and contact information are on the next page.

Onward and Cheers!
—Matt Knee

ABOUT THE AUTHOR

Matt Knee is the founder of MyCompanyWorks, Inc. (an INC5000 Company) which has helped over 50,000 entrepreneurs start and manage their business in all 50 states and DC. He's passionate about startups and has been helping entrepreneurs start and improve their companies since 2001. More importantly, Matt has seen (and made) every small business mistake in the book and is determined to make sure others don't make the same mistakes. He lives with his family in Las Vegas, Nevada.

Feedback and Resources:
Website: www.StartupsMadeSimple.com
Email: info@startupsmadesimple.com
Twitter: https://twitter.com/mattknee

APPENDIX

Recommended Reading

"Leaders are readers" as it's said. These are what I consider to be the best startup, management and personal effectiveness books (and essays). I recommend you read one new book each quarter (with your team if you have one).

- *1 Page Marketing Plan* by Allan Dib
- *7 Habits of Highly Effective People* by Stephen R. Covey
- *Getting Everything You Can Out of All You've Got* by Jay Abraham
- *Getting Things Done* by David Allen
- *Good to Great* by Jim Collins
- *No B.S. Ruthless Management of People and Profits* by Dan Kennedy
- *Scaling Up* by Verne Harnish
- *The E-Myth Revisited* by Michael E. Gerber
- *The Essential Drucker* by Peter F. Drucker
- *The Four Steps to the Epiphany* by Steve Blank
- *The Lean Startup* by Eric Ries
- *The New One Minute Manager* by Ken Blanchard
- *The One Minute Manager Meets the Monkey* by Ken Blanchard, William Oncken, Jr., and Hal Burrows
- *The Ultimate Sales Machine* by Chet Holmes
- *Traction* by Gino Wickman
- *Winning With Accountability* by Henry J. Evans
- *Work the System* by Sam Carpenter

Essays and Tweets by Naval Ravikant: https://twitter.com/naval
Essays by Paul Graham: http://www.paulgraham.com/articles.html

CPSIA information can be obtained
at www.ICGtesting.com
Printed in the USA
LVHW082352200420
653953LV00012BA/1098